POWER
OF *Nisa*

By: **Nidhi Gogia (Agarwal)**

AuthorHouse™ UK
1663 Liberty Drive
Bloomington, IN 47403 USA
www.authorhouse.co.uk
UK TFN: 0800 0148641 (Toll Free inside the UK)
UK Local: 02036 956322 (+44 20 3695 6322 from outside the UK)

Because of the dynamic nature of the Internet, any web addresses or links contained in this book may have changed
since publication and may no longer be valid. The views expressed in this work are solely those of the author and do not
necessarily reflect the views of the publisher, and the publisher hereby disclaims any responsibility for them.

Any people depicted in stock imagery provided by Getty Images are models,
and such images are being used for illustrative purposes only.
Certain stock imagery © Getty Images.

This book is printed on acid-free paper.

ISBN: 978-1-7283-7498-7 (sc)
ISBN: 978-1-7283-7497-0 (e)

Print information available on the last page.

Published by AuthorHouse 09/06/2022

Meaning of the Title

The word Nisa in Arabic means "women" the title represents the "power of women" who have fought for themselves and their rights.

Target Audience:

Women are the soft target, but victims do not have any gender. They need someone to listen to them. We're all victimised in some way; these stories will give you the courage to learn and understand your life's value.

Note: Some authentic Indian words have been used in the stories to maintain the vibes, check the glossary at the end of the book for the meaning. Glossary has been done chapter wise for easy navigation.

FIRST HAND IMPRESSIONS FROM THE EARLY READERS

Book Reviews by the people who read the book in its initial stages (before publication)

"Nidhi has been a friend and inspiration to me ever since I first met her several years ago, and this book reflects her sincere interest in women's lives, and determination to empower us to overcome the many challenges we face in the 21st century. A worthy endeavour, certainly, but the important messages are presented in such highly entertaining stories that you will find yourself wanting to read 'just one more' before you have to go and deal with one of the myriad tasks demanded of the modern woman!"

 # Catherine Dale (London, UK)

"This topic (power of women) and sexism in general has been more in and around the media in recent times yet it still sometimes goes under the radar and this book brilliantly portrays the issues that women face daily and intriguingly explains complex matters through short stories and poems and that's what is so brilliant about it. It was especially nice to see the work behind the scenes and the passion from the author and everyone involved to make this as good as possible."

#Abeer Gogia (London, UK)

"Thought provoking stories, largely genderless and the topics which need a shout out as these issues still exist in the 21st century. I loved each and every aspect of this book be it the story, poem or the moral. I will be recommending this book at my son's school and will be donating the copies myself to the school's library, once published, so our younger generation have an open access to this book and learn how to support the victims and raise their voice against any injustice which might be happening in their surroundings."

#Neha Gupta (New Delhi, India)

"As the Sketch artist of this book, I read the draft copy of the book to get the feel of the characters to portray them as close to the author's imagination of these real-life 16 women. Although I feel that I am privileged to be born in a family where there is no gender discrimination, seeing women and young girls suffering in the society around me, even in 21st century, always hurt me. This book has given me the strength and power to speak up productively for the empowerment of women and taught me to raise my voice for those who might not be as blessed as I am as we all should have access to the basic human rights, I am only talking here about the right to live!"

#Vishuddhi Jain, Sketch Artist (New Delhi, India)

"Nidhi's book is a peep into issues plaguing women in current times. The book is filled with stories that are not only of suffering, but of how these extraordinary women have succeeded in building a better life for themselves. Thus, the stories are about the strength and resilience of women. One of my favourite stories is the one about domestic abuse. It is an example of how women stand in solidarity with each other just like the maid's question inspires an epiphany in the abused making her question her situation. I am glad to have the opportunity of working on this book because being a woman there is nothing more satisfying than telling the narrative of most women in our society today."

#Aindrila Chandra, Illustration Artist (Kolkata, India)

"This book analyses the impact on the victim's mind and soul and how the orthodox society is suppressing the fundamental rights of women in India. The issues covered in this book are treated as everybody life in women's lives, but they're not. The book's title enticed me to understand and get to know the reality of the present condition of women in India."

#Afreen H. Warsi, Editor (Lucknow, India)

INDEX

ACKNOWLEDGMENT

Firstly, I would like to express my heartfelt gratitude to my brothers, Nikhil and Yash, who always support me in my passion. At the beginning of my journey as an author, when nobody believed in me, they stood by my side.

Nikhil has contributed his support to this book through his excellent poems for the characters with a special place in my heart.

Abeer, my son, cooked numerous meals on his own to give me time for my writing, so thank you, Abeer. He was always available to read the first draft of each chapter and to provide his valuable suggestions.

I cannot express the countless sacrifices of my parents, Mr. Ram Kumar Agarwal and Mrs. Manju Agarwal, in words. I am who I am because of my parents. I thank my dad for keeping a sharp eye on me; so, I don't get distracted during my writing journey to keep the book's progress on track.

I thank my sister, Neha, who was always ready to listen to my storylines. It was not difficult for her to understand various characters as she is the epitome of women empowerment herself. Special thanks to Abhishek, my brother-in-law, for always motivating me to speak up against injustice and to be that man in my life, who always supports the women in his life, be it his wife, sister, mother, mother-in-law, or sister-in-law.

Sadhvi and Catherine, my best friends, always inspired me to write this book, so thanks to them for believing in me and being on call anytime I was frustrated and distracted.

A big vote of thanks goes to my niece, Vishuddhi Jain, the Sketch artist of this book. This 13 year's child deserves special applause for sparing her valuable time for discussion about my characters, my imagination of those characters to fit the storyline, and to sketch and amend as necessary.

I am grateful to my entire family and friends.

It wouldn't be possible if I had not chosen myself over anyone else and met these strong women on each visit to India. I found myself in them, and the power we all shared has connected us.

I believe that if we consider Author as a body, then the editor is the backbone. Considering this analogy, I sincerely thanks to my editor, Ms. Afreen.H. Warsi. I am sincerely thankful to Afreen for not only editing the book but also for our conversations whenever clouds of confusion surrounded me.

I would also like to express my gratitude to AuthorhouseUk for their sincere efforts to publish this book and to my Publishing consultants, Paul Nicholas and May Arado, for answering my numerous emails in a timely fashion.

INTRODUCTION

My purpose of writing this book

I have gone through a phase in my life where I couldn't share my feelings and thoughts with anyone. It was always a feeling that Why is it only me?

From tolerance to fighting back, the journey was not easy, so I used to read books on women and watch movies where women are told and suppressed by a society that they're born to be treated like this, and it's normal. All I could see in those movies and books was a victim like me.

I'd realized nothing was normal around me; why was I victimizing myself when I always had the courage to speak for the wrongdoers?

It was my life lesson that gave me the courage to stand up for myself, rather than plead or degrade by someone who doesn't add value to my life.

I found the purpose of my life again, rebuilding my confidence, self-respect, self-love, and happiness.

I always wanted to write a book of short stories that give victims a crux of life where not everything can be fulfilled, but still a sense of accomplishment is felt, so here I present 'POWER OF NISA', short stories of 16 strong young girls and women who caught my attention on my various visits to India. Each story is a real-life story of a woman, I wanted this book to be the lighthouse to other woman struggling with one or the other issues I've covered in my first book. This is a Non-fiction book with names of the characters changed to maintain privacy of their lives though I've tried to keep the places same where I met them so as to keep the vibes flowing.

Nidhi Gogia

Myself, Nidhi Gogia, a British citizen of Indian origin, a single mother and a social media enthusiast to spread inspiration and motivation to the fellow women on how to deal with the regressive society and become an epitome of progression by taking control of their lives in their own hands. I am a professionally qualified Chartered and a Management Accountant who has a passion for educating others and transform lives and working as a Senior lecturer in Accounting and Finance at one of the top 40 Universities in UK.

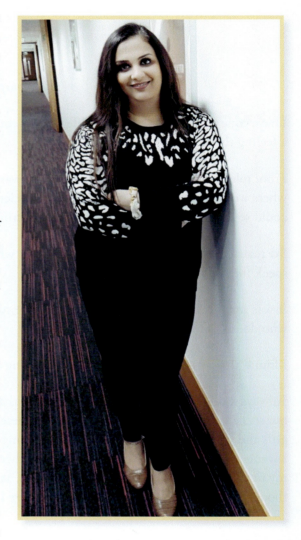

I am deeply intrigued by women issues in patriarchal society and have always wonder why women have to face so many adversities some of which makes me sick to the bottom of my stomach. I myself have been the victim of acute body shaming in my teenage years and throughout my adult life, I have been in a loveless marriage, suffered domestic violence and abuse, so I have not written this book without any understanding of what it takes to be the victim of one of the issues mentioned in the book. However, what I've realised over the years is that us women, we have to put our foot down to say 'enough is enough'. They can only victimise us till the time we believe we are the victims. May be the issues I have suffered are not serious at all compared to what some other women might be going through but nevertheless being severely harassed on a daily basis left scars not only on my heart and mind but my soul was pierced as well resulting in social anxiety, depression and a feeling of self-worthlessness, which is not acceptable to live a peaceful life.

I came out of it as I was Strong headed with determination to survive and I did set my mind in the correct direction of self-love and meditation.

I took this initiative to spread awareness among the fellow women through my linked in handle (www.linkedin.com/in/nidhi-gogia-aajkinaari) and there was no come back. Through Linked in, I was invited as a Guest speaker at a TREACH online event to talk on 'Underrepresentation of woman due to lack of education' which was a huge success with more than 50 worldwide audiences joining online and 100 more listening to the recorded podcast. Soon after the event, on the special request of some of the audiences, I started my You tube channel (https://www.youtube.com/c/AajKiNaaribyNidhiGogia) to keep spreading awareness, positivity and motivation on a regular basis through my thought provoking videos in different styles and formats and one of the format widely loved are the short stories with the moral. And hence, I decided to format my 1st book in the same format, making it interesting to read though genderless and ageless.

I would like to work more and better to support minority (underprivileged) to live up to their abilities in society.

Nikhil Agarwal

I'm a Chartered Accountant by profession. I'm engaged in my family business for living. I started writing poems 5 years ago as a hobby. Soon it became my passion. When I received an offer to become a part of this project "POWER OF NISA", I couldn't resist such a wonderful opportunity. I have written the introductory poem and the one at the end of this book. I have also covered 3 stories and tried to portray these as poems. Plus, my poem on the hardship of single parents is very close to my heart. I hope you all will have a good time reading this book

POWER FORCE OF 'POWER OF NISA'

1. *Afreen H. Warsi,* EDITOR

Never underestimate the power of 'Karma'. A child who hates writing a 200-word essay never knew that she'd fall in love, and then a heartbreak will get her closer to the one she hated writing; that's how I got closer to the words than the world. I chose my symphony of life in words; later, I got addicted to writing not every day but on my most sad days, when I felt emptiness and loneliness. Those writings turned into professional writing and editing blogs and content for websites now editing a book.

And when I got the opportunity to edit 'Power of Nisa' and Author Nidhi described her perspective about this book, I didn't give it a second thought as I felt connected with each character. While editing, I lived each pain and moment of the story characters and realised they could have chosen suicide, but women are like water; they make their own way. Thank you, Nidhi, for choosing me and making me a part of these powerful thoughts.

2. *Aindrila Chandra,* ILLUSTRATION ARTIST

I am a self-taught artist and digital illustrator who loves to bring ideas from the mind into reality.

My journey in art had started early in childhood and it has continued to intrigue me to this day. From doodling at the back of notebooks during boring classes to learning from online resources to pursuing art as a professional, I still see myself as a work in progress.

This project was an enlightening experience which brought me closer to the sufferings of women from all walks of life. I hope my illustrations would help the readers sympathise with those sufferings and they would strive to build a better society.

3. *Vishuddhi Jain,* SKETCH ARTIST

I am Vishuddhi Jain, a 13-year-old student from New Delhi, India. I am a budding artist and this is my first ever published work as a sketch artist and I am proud to have started early as this is just the beginning....

Painting is my passion. I see it in every scene of nature. Its vivid colours fill my imagination with fantasies which I try to bring to life through my art.

ART IS MY LIFE!!

Nidhi Mausi (my mum's bff) has already contracted me for her next project and I am on cloud 9. I still remember the day when she offered this project to me, my mummy was convinced that this will give me an opportunity to learn but I was anxious as I never did sketching before and I was sort of scared of getting these sketches published but Nidhi mausi and mummy got me convinced and I am happy I did listen to my elders, I learnt a lot through each and every sketch I did for this project, some sketches were done multiple times to reflect the characters as portrayed in the stories but its all for the good! Thank you Nidhi mausi for believing in me when even I did not believe in myself, I would like to dedicate the start of my Sketch artist career to you!!

Today's world: what our Nisa have to face: through the eyes of our home poet

A WOMAN

I am a woman,
I give birth,
To a new generation,
I give birth,
To men & women,
Incomplete is every male,
Without the existence of a female.

Why do I face a cruel practice,
Before my birth, I'm murdered,
I'm murdered & killed in this practice,
Female foeticide is a brutal practice.
Female foeticide inside a female,
Can you reproduce without a female?

I'm not a toy to play,
I'm not a property to own,
In my childhood, why get I raped,
Unknowing the meaning of rape,
Child sexual abuse is itself rape.

I'm considered the goddess of wealth,
Why don't you think about my health?
I want to play in my nonage,
But burden I get in my nonage,
Household chores I get at this age,
Child marriage in my nonage,
Pregnancy in my teenage.

Sometimes I fall in the wrong hands,
I love him, so I hold his hands,
He pushed me in whoring,
With his own hands.

Sometimes I'm sold without my wish,
As if I'm golden fish,
I'm not an asset but I'm sold,
In a profession which is old,
As old as this, mankind is old.
As a slave, I'm used,
From antiquity, I'm being abused.

Sometimes, I'm forced to work,
In my hands, loads of work,
To fill up the pockets,
I'm forced to work,
Instead of books,
In my hands, loads of work,
Instead of school,
As child labour, I have to work,
As slave labour, I have to work.

Sometimes, I refuse,
Refuse to accept,
Accept a proposal,
As I love someone else,
As I like someone else,
I have a crush on someone else,

I have to pay a price for refusal,
Attack on my beauty for such a refusal,
Attack on my face, for such a refusal,
Attack on solemnity, for such a refusal
Attack on my dignity, for such a refusal,
An acid attack, for such a refusal.

Is it a crime for refusing someone?
Is it a crime to love someone?
If it is not, why do I pay for a refusal?
I can't see myself in the mirror,
The payment by me is a social mirror.

Sometimes, I produce sterile eggs,
But I want to stand on my legs,
My family taunt, society taunt,
A baby bump, I cannot flaunt,
Don't I have a right to live?
I can't produce a baby to live.

Sometimes, I'm referred,
As a man-eater, a culpable woman,
A witch, a malicious woman,
A cannibal, I'm referred,

What's my fault if, my man has died,
I'm starved because my better half died,
I'm referred to an escort, my spouse died,
Can't I have the right to live?
Just because my groom died.

I'm raising my voice against these evils,
Many are the victim of these evils,
Male dominance is a social evil,
Society has to stand against these evils,
I can't produce a girl with these evils.

CHAPTER 1:

AAJ KI NAARI

Always remember the power and courage lies within us, we just need to discover it!
#Anonymous

<u>Snapshot</u>

She gained what she has never lost.

Yes, Sargam did every possible thing to adjust and compromise in her marriage life.

While adjusting, she forgot the meaning of self-respect and let her husband torture her throughout, emotionally, financially and physically.

She was said to be ugly, fat, and a shame for their family, and she believed all this; Sargam started living with this emotional baggage.

But why are only women taught to sacrifice and adjust in their in-law's house? Isn't in-laws' responsibility to make her feel comfortable and learn about her favourite too?

Why do women like Sargam tolerate all this?

Character sketch

Main Character's description

Sargam is in her early 40s, resides in London, UK, and is a professional Chartered Accountant and a social media enthusiast hoping to spread positivity, love and laughter.

She is not so tall, not short though, wheatish, long hair, big eyes with dark circles and a bit overweight but always full of confidence and knows how to smile in adversities. She is a ray of positivity to many.

Story

It was summer in London, and the stadium was full of football fans; It was a match between Argentina and Italy. People were excited, and the match was about to begin. My son Hetansh took me along with him. It has been decades that I avoided large gatherings, but I went for Hetansh's happiness. I was hesitant and anxious about seeing too many people under one roof, but Hetansh held my hand and made me seated.

Soon, the match started, and Messi scored a goal! Wembley was echoed with Messi, Messi! and the girl sitting beside me jumped in excitement from her seat, and she even made me stand along with her. She held my hand and started dancing, shouting and shaking her head happily.

I was looking at her face and saw my reflection in her, that twenty-year-old Sargam, carefree, relaxed with short hairs, wheatish complexion, small built with good height and big eyes.

My eyes were the most attractive physical feature; big, sparkling, and full of joy. The extrovert Sargam was full of ambition; she was intelligent and outspoken.

Sargam was popularly known for spreading happiness and making everyone laugh.

Back to the match, she hugged me and left my hand, we sat down again, and the stadium became all quiet, waiting for the next goal to happen.

But I was lost in my past. It was a bright sunny day when I first met Kartik, son of my dad's friend, at Gants Hills railway station in Ilford.

His parents sent some gifts for him from India. I gave that to him, and then we said goodbye. After that meeting, we started texting each other. It wasn't like I loved him, but I liked chatting with him daily.

I was studying Professional accounting, and he was doing his MBA. We were both in different universities, so we planned to go on weekend day trips. Those weekend trips made us good friends. We often planned such trips, and this is how two years passed by in London. My studies got completed soon after that I got a good job.

Kartik always praised me for being ambitious and encouraged me to fulfil my goals. His husky voice got my attention. If we did not talk on the phone even for a day, I used to feel strange, as if something was incomplete.

And that's how we got to know we love each other without telling it officially.

One day Kartik said do you know Sargam? We do not match each other. I'm too handsome, and look at yourself; you're wheatish, short hair with dark circles. My parents will never accept a daughter-in-law like you. You do not match my level of looks. You're ugly.

I was quiet and listening to Kartik. These comments made me sad, but I didn't want to lose Kartik.

He started criticising me every day for my studies, my job, looks, decisions, and on my ambitions.

I asked myself, *"Why am I stretching this relationship? I should leave Kartik."*

But I was madly in love with Kartik. I thought of sacrificing each thing for him. I did not realise I was the only one making all the effort in this relationship.

After one year of our relationship, my family called me to say they were looking for a guy in India, but I told them about Kartik.

My family was against this relationship because of our caste differences. I'm Baniya, and he was Punjabi. Kartik's educational and financial status were part of their concerns, too, where I was a lecturer, and he was a waiter, but somehow I convinced my family to get me married to Kartik.

Even Kartik's family said No because, according to his family, I was not pretty or fair.

Kartik called me angrily and said, *"Sargam, why are you so ugly? Why don't you go to the parlour and put on makeup to look good? I'm ashamed of you."*

I just cried on the phone and asked, "But Kartik, you were aware of how I look, how I eat, and how I dress up, and why are you saying all this?

I was utterly shattered and sad at Kartik's rudeness towards me.

Kartik didn't receive my calls for two days, and I was still thinking of marrying him as I was blindfolded in love with him.

I had an option of leaving him for disrespecting me and discouraging me, but I chose Kartik over anything, which, now thinking about it, was very wrong.

After some months of struggling and convincing, Kartik and I got married. I was happy that everything had fallen in place now. Little did I know that it was just the beginning of my ordeal, not the beginning of a fairy tale like I had always dreamt of.

It was my wedding night when I was waiting for Kartik in our room. He came, and he was on a call with his mother when she said, *" I still can't believe that such an ugly girl is my daughter-in-law."*

They both laughed at this. It was enough to break my self-esteem.

After keeping the call, Kartik came and beat me ruthlessly. He said, *"You're a black spot in my life. Now my friends will laugh at me because of you."*

And, he left me on the floor weeping the whole night, which continued for three years. I let him abuse me and torture me mentally, emotionally, and physically.

But I realised it's not love anymore; we were just living our lives. I was scared to divorce as I married Kartik against my family's will. They gave permission but never consented fully to this relationship like they sensed this early on!

I was with him but alone. His mother pointed out that I can't keep his son happy, so I should welcome his girlfriends to my bedroom.

He had many extramarital affairs in the name of *"we're just friends."*

I woke up one day when I tested my pregnancy, and it was positive. I was like, seriously! God, is it true? Just for my relief, I checked my result ten times and was over the moon and shared this news with Kartik.

I guess those nine months of my pregnancy were a relief after three years. Everything was going well when Kartik's mother started convincing him to abort this child as they didn't want their grandchild to be wheatish and ugly just like the child's mother; it was the fifth month, but surprisingly, Kartik said to his mother that he wants this child to be born. That was a big relief to me. Although I had decided I'll not abort my child for them, I felt good when I was not forced to argue with him on this matter. He stopped beating me frequently but still curses me, my looks and my family daily.

I had a painful pregnancy too. I thought Kartik would look after me now that he might change his behaviour towards me, but I lost five kilograms during my pregnancy.

He was least concerned about my health. I cooked my own meals after coming from work. Sometimes I even slept hungrily.

Finally, Hetansh, my little bundle of joy, was born, but nothing changed. I was still beaten regularly; after some time, we started sleeping in different rooms. He didn't help me once in the upbringing of our son.

I was body-shamed regularly, and Kartik used to see me with hatred and disgust. And it was Hetansh's third birthday when his family came for dinner.

Kartik got into a fight with me; then his mother said, *"Slap her; that's the only way she understands."*

That day I saw Hetansh was watching us; I held Kartik's hand and said, *"now it's over; you can't beat me, abuse me or body shame me. I'm leaving you and your ugly family."*

I was crying and saying all this. It was my frustration of years that I let go. I don't want Hetansh to become like you. You can't shut my mouth again by hitting me. I regret to be your wife, but I won't regret it now

I took Hetansh and walked off the house. We stayed in a hotel for three months, and a new me made a decision for herself now. I filed a case against Kartik, and we fought legally for our rights and property, of which I owned 50%.

I did not realise when I became so brave. I didn't want anything extra from Kartik. I want to get out of that abusive relationship and give a loving upbringing to Hetansh. I knew I could not be his dad, but I wanted him to believe in relations and love.

It's been ten years now that we parted ways. I never stopped Kartik from meeting his son. But with time, Kartik remarried, and he stopped visiting Hetansh now.

We sometimes talk on the phone as friends from where we started.

And it was another goal by Argentina again she held my hand. This time, I was dancing, too, as now I am living a happy and contented normal life with my son Hetansh, and I know I deserve the peace and respect I craved in that abusive relationship. This dance was not only to celebrate that winning goal but to celebrate my life and how far I've come alone, and the best part is I've raised a good man; Hetansh is a good child, and I am proud of him as a mother!

With time I realised how important it is to be your own self and never plead for love. I was, and I'm comfortable in my skin and gained my confidence again.

I don't need anyone's opinion to tell me about my looks and life. I'm alone as a warrior.

Always remember, *When you are not included, invited, or considered, whisper to yourself.*

"Thank you for the space necessary in my life for the people who matter most to me. I am blessed."

Moral of the story

Body shaming is criticising, humiliating and bullying someone on the basis of their body shape, size, appearance, looks, age etc.

Can be done by?
- Parents

- Siblings

- Friends

- Family members

- Neighbours

- Classmates at school/ College

- Office colleagues

- Enemies

Effects on the victim?
- Mental and emotional trauma

- Low self esteem

- Anger

- Eating disorders

- Sleeping disorders

- Depression

- Self- harm

- Mental health disorders

- Social anxiety

How to overcome it?
- Stick up to yourself in a positive and healthy way.

- Confront the body shamer and if its not safe, leave the place immediately.

- SELF- LOVE and do not let negative comments bother you. You do not have to listen to everything everyone has to say, you don't have to care.

- If you believe you're indeed overweight, try to reduce the weight for health reasons, not just to fit in with the society.

- Body shaming on social media can be reported and flagged up through NEDA (National Eating Disorder Association).

- Engage and do social networking with strong and positive individuals.

PLEASE REMEMBER THAT YOU MAY BODY SHAME SOMEONE AS A JOKE FOR A LAUGHTER FOR A FRACTION OF SECONDS BUT THE LASTING EFFECTS OF BODY SHAMING ARE NO LAUGHING MATTER!!!

To wind it up with **Oprah's** powerful quote:

"Step away from the mean girls and say bye- bye to feeling bad about your looks. Are you ready to stop colluding with a culture that makes so many of us feel physically inadequate? Say goodbye to your inner critic, and take this pledge to be kinder to yourself and others"

Sargam's story from the perspective of our home poet

The adorable eyes, the talkative eyes,
The garrulous eyes, the expressive eyes,
The black hairs, the slim body,
But not with, a skinny body,
A talkative girl, a chatterbox,
I was an ordinary girl.
I was a common girl.

I saw a dream,
An ambition to study,
I moved to a city,
For an ambition to study.

The city was the dream city,
It was the central city,
A multi-city, within the city,
It was a clock city.

I connected with a guy,
As I had a few things,
Things to deliver, to this guy,
The sweet was the guy,
So, I made a friend, this guy,
I started talking to this guy,
As I was,
A chatterbox,
So, we met a few times,
It was my loneliness every time,
My emptiness every time.

Slowly-slowly, I drown in love,
My heart fell, fell in love,
There was a problem in my love,
I was a plain-looking girl,
A common girl, an ordinary girl.

I thought it was love,
All he wanted was a beautiful love,
He didn't know what was love,
His eyes always wanted a lustful love.

He had been a critic to me,
He always commented,
On the skin of me,
The colour of me,

The face of me,
In his eyes, I was an ugly girl,
I was a plain-looking girl,
A common girl, an ordinary girl.

Just before the night of marriage,
He just showed off his colours,
He just told me,
What he always thought,
His parents were against the marriage,
Just before the night of marriage,
He just showed who he was,
Just before the night of marriage.

Just before the night of marriage,
My parents too, were against the marriage,
Because they know the norms of marriage,
The repercussions of this marriage,

He was a no match to me,
His degrees were no match to mine,
His society was no match to mine,
He was a no match to me,
I continued the marriage,
Because there was a loneliness in me,
An emptiness in me forced me,
To continue the marriage.

I tried to love,
With all my soul,
To change these things,
To control things is,
All I was aiming,
What all I got,
Was body shaming,
Not just from him,
But from his family too.

The clock ticked away,
The time passed by,
All I got was,
Many affairs from him.
Diffidence from him,
Taunting from him.

These were reduced,
When I was pregnant,
But all I lacked was,
The focus from him,
The attention from him,
The love from him.

During the period of 9 months,
I got the taunts that,
My baby would be ugly,
Ugly like me,
Get it to abort,
Was his mom's demand,
She didn't want,
An ugly newborn,
During those 9 months.

He never paid attention,
Attention to me,
About the meals,
The meals of me,
About health,
The health of me,
During those 9 months.
The day then came,
When Hetansh was born,
He was the gift,
Presented to me,
For carrying him,
In the womb of me,
During the 9 months.

I started to sleep,
In the separate room,
With my gift,
Mamma and baby,
Both in the room.

Three years had now passed,
It was his birthday, his third birthday,
We went to dinner, on his third birthday,
My in-laws were there, on this birthday,

His mom asked,
Asked him to slap,
A slap on my face,

A slap was an ace,
To shut my face.

I hold his hand, in the air,
I had overcome,
Overcome my fear,
I had dried,
Dried up my tears,
I decided to resist,
This intrusion of fear,
In front of my baby dear.

All I thought,
We were a team,
But it was an attack,
On my self-esteem.

All I had was enough,
Enough was enough,
The taunting was enough,
Body shaming was enough.

I decided to move on,
From this relationship,
A toxic one,
A venomous one,
A noxious one.

All I knew,
I had to fight a long battle,
In the court of law, a long battle,
To secure the wealth,
Half of the wealth,
To secure the hereafter,
My kid's hereafter.

What an irony it was,
Where I moved,
A hotel, it was,
What I left,
My home, it was,
Where I fought,
The court, it was,
For what I fought,
My home, it was,
Why I fought,

For my kid, it was,
How I fought,
With my courage, it was,
We were separated,
We were separated.

Now he is married,
Married to a lady,
A beautiful lady,
Fulfilled his dreams,
Of a beautiful lady.

I never denied,
Denied to him,
To talk to his son,
To meet his son,
But these are the things,
Which are rarely done.

Now I talk to him,
As friends talk,
Exchange our words,
Like we used to do,
Before falling in love.

Now I believe,
It is the best,
The best finish,
That I can expect,
With this relationship.

All I have the words,
The Words to share,
Share with the readers,
When you place,
Place your love,
Above your dignity,
Sooner or later,
It is inevitable,
Sooner or later,
It is inevitable,

I have the courage,
To tell you my story,
But many stories,
The similar stories,
Remain like untold stories.

CHAPTER 2:

SCREAM OF THE NIGHTMARE

"For the perpetrator, rape lasts just a matter of minutes. For the victim it never stops."
~Fredrick Backman (Beratown (Beartown, #1))

<u>Snapshot</u>

Rape is a crime. Don't treat victims as culprits.

Kanak was passionate; she wanted to pursue her dreams and fought for herself to get admission to a big city.

But what makes people think if a girl is living alone and bold, she has no respect or character?

That's what happened with Kanak; while believing in her dreams, she started believing in people too.

She didn't know that being a victim, she'll be criticized for being a woman.

Character Sketch

Main Character's Description

Kanak is now a 23-year-old firm and bold girl with short hair and a beautiful body.

A passionate writer who dresses up powerfully and earns for her livelihood. A tall wheatish girl with a slim body and sharp facial features.

Story

Mom, don't worry! I have reached Delhi. I have taken a room. The PG's family is very humble, caring, and loving. Uncle Raj and aunt Sharmila have no children. So, there will be no child to annoy me during my studies—all set. "I will go to my college tomorrow", *Kanak said cheerfully.*

"I am your mother, dear. I will keep fearing for you. Be careful of the family and neighbours around you. You don't know who carries a devil's personality inside," mother replied anxiously.

"Oh, mom! Enough. I am 19 and capable of dealing with this world. Now don't irritate me by whispering the same words again and again."

"Fine. Take care. Mamma loves you."

Kanak's mother replied, "Love you too. Bye."

Kanak was excited because tomorrow would be the first day at her new college. She slept peacefully, woke up at 7.00 am, and got ready for college.

Kanak enjoyed herself a lot in her college. She got some smart teachers, amazing friends, and an idea of Delhi's pollution.

Kanak reached her PG at 5.00 pm. Her aunt welcomed her with a smile and asked, "How was your day, Kanak?"

"Amazing aunt, I am a bit tired, but yes, I took pleasure in it a lot," Kanak replied exhaustedly.

Raj and Sharmila asked Kanak to have her food at their home tonight. Kanak refused, but she finally got convinced for a dinner party.

Kanak was happy with her PG. She thought she would not miss her parents much. She found the environment homely and pleasant.

The next day Kanak's male friend came with her to drop her home. Meena, Kanak's neighbor, noticed Kanak with her male friend.

On the same night, Meena arrived at Sharmila's home to take sugar from her. But the main reason was to gossip about Kanak. Kanak, Sharmila, and Raj were talking in the same room when aunt Meena arrived.

Meena said, "Sharmila, how can you be so irresponsible in choosing a tenant for your home. A boy came up with Kanak to drop her home."

Kanak didn't say anything. She was put to shame for pretty normal stuff, and there was nothing wrong with it.

Raj replied angrily, "Everybody must change their thinking with time. Kanak was with her classmate. She is not aware of the Delhi metro routes properly. Grow up, Meena, you too have your own children to take care of."

Meena couldn't say anything and got out of the house in a rage. But Kanak was happy because at least someone took a stand for her. She thanked uncle Raj for understanding and supporting her.

The next day was similar to the previous day. When Kanak reached home, she learned that Sharmila's cousin had caught typhoid. She went to Noida to look after her cousin.

Kanak was tired, so she went to her room. The day was quite hot. She was taking a bath when she heard something ambiguous. It seemed like someone was outside the bathroom.

She shouted, "Who's there?" But no one answered. She thought it was a misconception.

She went to the kitchen to take some water. Raj was already present there.

Raj said, "Hi Kanak, how was your day?"

"Great uncle! I wanted water from the refrigerator."

"Oh! Sure." Raj took out a bottle and gave it to Kanak and asked if she had her lunch".

Kanak felt the warmth and happiness of choosing a good family.

She went to take a nap.

The door lock was broken. At 2.00 pm, Kanak heard some noises.

But she ignored it as she was tired and slept again.

At night Uncle Raj ordered pizza for him and Kanak.

Kanak was on a video call with her mother when Uncle Raj came to Kanak's room and knocked at the door.

Kanak asked, "Who's there?"

Uncle Raj "Kanak Beta, I've got a pizza for you." As aunt Sharmila is not home, I thought you might be hungry.

Kanak replied, "Thank you so much, uncle, for looking after me."

Uncle Raj "Goodnight, beta."

Kanak's mom thanks God for blessing their daughter with such a humble family.

But the noises happened again at midnight.

Kanak woke up in fear and shouted, "Who's there? I said, tell me, Who's there? '' I am gonna scream, I will call the police, I will call neighbours, tell me who's there."

But nobody answered. Kanak couldn't sleep the whole night.

She didn't want to tell her mother anything about yesterday's night. She was not getting permission from her father to take college outside her city, but her mother convinced him to do the same. She thought that she would have to go back to her hometown if her parents got to know something like that.

Kanak was hesitant to share the incident with Uncle Raj and decided to remain silent and wait for her aunt Sharmila to come.

It was Sunday. Sharmila's train was scheduled to arrive at 5.00 pm. At 7.00 am, Raj departed for his work.

Kanak then fell asleep in her room. She felt something on her neck; it was some human touch.

Kanak woke up and screamed, "Uncle, what are you doing? You are supposed to be at your work. Why are you here?"

Kanak miserably started finding her phone, but her phone was not on the table. The window was locked. She sensed the ambiguous situation.

She was crying, screaming for help. "Meena, aunt, uncle, please help. Raj, I said, get out of here. Now!" She was screaming for her life. But nobody was listening to her.

What we feared happened! Raj raped Kanak. Lying on the floor, thinking about her life coming to an end, Kanak was fighting and crying about her physical and mental condition. She was half dead.

"It seems somebody from Sharmila's home is shouting," said Brijesh, Meena's son.

"We don't have to take care of her home. Shut up and do your work", Meena yelled at her son.

"Mom, we can at least see what is happening. Who knows if there is some critical situation?"

Brijesh came out on his balcony. He saw from a little opening that Kanak was lying on the floor. He was quite intelligent to grasp the suspicious situation. Brijesh thought something was wrong. He immediately called the police.

As soon as the police reached Brijesh's home, he told the police about the whole event. The police decided to enter Raj's home secretively.

Raj was scared of a crime he did to Kanak. So, he decided to kill her and hide her dead body. He went down to bring a knife to kill Kanak.

The police caught Raj with a knife. One officer asked, "where were you taking this knife?"

"Nowhere, I was going to cut fruits for me," *Raj replied scarcely.*

The police then started finding other family members. The police reached Kanak's room, where Kanak was still lying on the floor, crying badly, not in the condition even to walk.

The whole matter opened up in front of the police. Kanak's parents were called to the situation. Sharmila also reached the spot later.

"I would not have kept this girl in my home. I know she has done something, and the blame is on my husband", Sharmila said angrily to save her status.

"Brijesh, you must come with us as a witness," said a police officer.

Meena replied, "Why, my son? I told you, Brijesh, not to give your head between other matters."

Kanak's parents couldn't do anything instead of crying their hearts out.

Kanak was silently and empty-mindedly listening to all the opinions. But she couldn't hold herself from speaking when she heard her parent's view.

Kanak's father said, "I told you not to send her to Delhi. You and your daughter don't listen to anyone. I can't call her my daughter anymore. I am ashamed of her."

"I should not have sent my little girl to this big brutal city. Mera bacha! It is my fault." Kanak's mother had no option left instead of sobbing.

"Papa, do you still think the fault is mine? Mamma, he raped me; is it my fault? Tell me. I came here for my studies, is it my fault? I wanted to become a journalist. I wanted to pursue my higher studies; is it my fault?"

"No! Not anymore."

"Mamma, Papa, it is your fault. You didn't form a friendly environment at home so that I could tell you about my miserable situation without any fear."

"It is society's fault that it can notice me with a boy, my classmate, but couldn't make any efforts to look at my home and investigate if everything was ok."

"If people like Brijesh had not existed, I would be here dying before you. That would be better, right? For all of you?" Kanak keeps saying with a heavy heart and rage in her eyes.

"Enough! I don't want your unpopular opinions. Enough!"

"Don't worry, dad. Don't call me your daughter. Mom! Don't cry anymore. Just think your girl is either dead or didn't exist."

And you, the so-called neighbours and Sharmila, don't make me feel ashamed about anything else. I will surely let Raj punish him for this heinous crime."

"I am capable enough to do a part-time job and pursue my further studies. I will live my life on my terms. I will recover from it. I neither want you all nor your unpopular opinions about me."

Kanak's eyes were red in rage. She moved out of that place with a decision to recover and work on herself, don't care about people anymore.

"Enough! Enough!" She moved out by uttering these words continuously.

She moved out, but the irony is even her parents did not stop or supported her. But Kanak stood for herself.

"I couldn't find any place in this tough city instead of your home. Please help me", said Kanak to his classmate Meet.

"Don't worry, Kanak. I will help you. You can stay in our guest house until you find some source of income."

"But your parents? Will they allow me to live here?"

"Don't worry! I talked to my parents when you called me. They agreed. They are educated and sensible enough to understand your condition."

"Thanks, Meet."

"You're welcome. Now just focus on your studies and finding a source of income for you."

"Sure, I will."

Kanak started living in her friend's house. She always wanted to become a journalist. Kanak had a passion for writing. She explored the internet to find some writing work for her. The first two months were struggling. She was doing unpaid internships to learn writing professionally. She avoided college for the first two months and closed herself in a room.

Kanak made her id on several social media channels with the name "Kanak, the survivor." She used to post her thoughts on those channels in her free time.

After two months, she got her first income from writing. She took a freelance project and earned "2000 INR."

"I did it—my first income. I can and I will", Kanak whispered to herself.

It was a small amount but huge for a little girl trying to survive alone, trying to be independent. It gave her confidence.

She came out of the house three months later and decided to take a step forward towards herself and left those "unpopular opinions" of people.

She started going to college. Stars started shining in Kanak's destiny. Her freelance income increased to "30,000 INR" in just one month.

"I will take a room on rent now. Thanks for your help. If you weren't there, I would not be capable of achieving all this", said Kanak to Meet.

"You are capable of achieving anything or everything."

Kanak started living in a rental room. She keeps writing, earning, and pursuing her further studies. Fortunately, people started loving her writing on social media channels. Within eight months, her income increased.

Kanak decided to break all the bars and tell her story to the people. She made a video on how she survived her rape journey, then abandoned by society, fought for herself, overcame her mental conditions, and lived like a queen. She uploaded the video on her social media handles.

Overnight, her story got famous, and people started engaging with her video.

"How shameful? After being raped, she is in front of the camera and uttering this shameful stuff in front of the whole world."

"Another way of gaining popularity. Grow up, girl. It is not the correct way to gain favour."

"Raped and still normal. A liar!"

"So, you earn by letting people rape you? Please give me a chance."

These were the comments of a few people on her video. Yes. Few! Because the majority of comments were in favour of Kanak.

"Glad you came up with this. We are with you."

"I am also an acid attack survivor. Sad that your parents are not with you. My parents supported me a lot. Now, I work at Amazon prime as a casting director."

"I also got raped once. But I do not have the courage to overcome it and live my life on my terms. You motivated me a lot. Now, I also will find some way of earning and get independent and do something for my NGO."

But one comment brought a big smile to Kanak's face.

What was that?

Wait, it was her father's comment:

"It is not your fault, it was never your fault that you got raped. I am ashamed of myself, but I am proud of you, my daughter, *Mera bachcha, Kanak!*"

Moral of the story

BE STRONG even though that scene might always haunt you, you might not forget your screams at that moment, 'mummy', 'mummy', 'papa', 'papa', 'save me', 'leave me', 'no, no, noooooo…….'.

Please focus on emotions like love, Joy, Peace to come out of fear and anxiety. Meditate daily (or if not possible daily, regularly) to find peace and to heal from the trauma. Remember, healing is not forgetting that ugly demon and what he did to you/ with you, it is to learn how to live peacefully and to move on.

You will never forget his smell and I am sure you will still panic and frighten in dark, if you are alone but ALWAYS REMEMBER, IT WAS NOT YOUR FAULT THAT HE WAS SICK AND HE DID THAT TO YOU. IT WAS NOT YOUR FAULT THAT YOU WERE ALONE THAT DAY. IT WAS NOT YOUR FAULT THAT YOU WERE WEARING A SKIRT THAT NIGHT AND TOOK A CAB ALONE, HE WOULD HAVE DONE IT EVEN IF YOU WERE DRAPED IN A 6 YARD SAREE as the fault lies in his sick mentality, not in your clothes.

Parents: Instead of putting restrictions on your girls (on their clothes, timings, body language etc), educate your sons to respect the girls and not to see them as a sex object. They need to learn the boundaries and know that raping a woman is not acceptable leave alone forcing sex on someone saying 'No'. Education starts at home, do not be ashamed of talking about these matters with your children when they are teenagers. Do not make sex a taboo so your kids are fascinated about it and the opposite gender. The more we hide it, the more our kids will be involved with pornography etc which results in these crimes at the end. Talk about it, create an open space in your family where your kids can ask you questions

Victims: The day you will be able to tell your story to others without crying will be the day of your revenge, not only from him but from the society as well. Our society needs a wake-up call by not trying to be regressive by making it look like it was actually your fault. Majority of these rape cases are not even reported as that might bring shame to the family and this is what these sick men know and take benefit of and get away with their horrendous act. Speak up, not only for you, but for the other innocent victims as well. Together, we can make it happen!

Work hard to achieve your dreams. That one crime cannot set you back, they might have crushed your soul but do not let them crush your dreams. FLY, you can still fly high like you could do before that night. Your world might have changed from 'before' to 'after' in a fraction of minutes, trust me, he raped you, **it was not your fault**, there was nothing wrong with you then and there is nothing wrong with you now.

Rape is brutal, DO NOT BRUSH OFF THINGS UNDER THE CARPET.

As SIR MARTIN LUTHER KING, JR, rightly quoted:
"Our lives begin to end the day we become silent about things that matter."

Kanak's story from the perspective of our home poet

I had my dreams,
Dreams, not so big,
I wanted to study,
As adolescents do.

I wanted to fly,
If the skies were mine.
I didn't know, my feathers,
My feathers would be pierced.

I came to the city,
To study in the city,
So I searched for a place,
A shelter in the city.

I found a shelter,
A shelter in the city,
The owner was sweet,
But I was unaware,
About his mask.

One day,
When I was alone,
When he was alone,
He took off his mask,
When we were alone.

He just showed his real face,
He just left his human race,
Because he was of a monster race,
He was of a predator race.

He invaded me, molested me,
Abducted me, violated me,
Abused me, spoiled me,
I was robbed. not just me,
But my dignity and dreams too,
I trusted him, so my trust too.

My feathers got pierced,
My eyes got teared,
On that single day,
My life's black day,
I was raped,
Yes, I was raped,
On that day.

I was unconscious,
For the number of days,
The dilemma was so fierce,
I couldn't recall,
The number of days.

Opened my eyes in the dawn of my life,
Full of quizzes, so the dawn was,
Had to cross, the dawn of quizzes,
I desired to live but had to cross the quizzes.

So many eyes were questioning me,
And my character was the only me,
I became a toy, so my soul was,
I became soulless, so my character was.

Even my creators had doubtful optics,
Their eyes were trying to make me guilty,
Their speech had already made me guilty,
But in my eyes, humanity was guilty.

I pledged to fight,
As hard as I could,
I studied hard,
As hard as I could,
To uplift myself,
And those who need,
To do some deeds,
To do good deeds.

Because of the deeds,
I became the voice,
Of those in need,
Now society is proud of me,
So, my parents are,
Now I can't see the questioning mouths,
The abusing mouths.

Now I pen down,
Pen down the stories,
The similar tales,
As of mine,
I pen down poems,
As I did,
As I did.

CHAPTER 3:

LITTLE DID I KNOW

"Any young man, who makes dowry a condition to marriage, discredits his education and his country and dishonours womanhood." #Mahatma Gandhi

<u>Snapshot</u>

All heroes don't wear capes.

Yes, Rukhsar's father treated her like a princess; gave her the wings to fly high.

He made her dream come true, even letting her marry the man she loves, Shayan, her dream.

She was happy and excited like any ordinary girl on her wedding day with butterflies in her tummy, but she did not know what was coming next.

A man who promised Rukhsar a happy life had put a condition for her happiness before their Nikah.

Character Sketch

Character description

Rukhsar is in her late 20s now. She is a pretty hijabi Muslim girl who believes in living in a moment with long brunette sleek hair and a diamond face shape.

She is 5'5, and a bit healthy, but her glowing, flawless skin makes her look prettier.

Story

It was November 15, 2020. I woke up with a bright smile and a glow on my face and said to myself finally; the big day has arrived; yay, I'm so happy.

I could sense the warmth and happiness in every corner of my house. All my cousins slept in my room on the floor, and it was so much fun, and I realized I was going to miss all these things. The relations are going to change. These feelings made me a bit nervous, but I knew Shayan would make me feel comfortable. That thought gave me confidence.

"*Halwai*" was preparing breakfast for the guests. My mother came to me and fed me poori sabzi and said this is the last day of your carefree life, and we both laughed hysterically. My father was serving jalebi to my uncle and was sharing a great laugh.

The day was passing in a rush. My cousin's dress was not fitting properly, someone's sandals were not matching, and the chaos was going on with stress and happiness in parallel.

As the clock was ticking, my heartbeats increased, and I was experiencing mixed emotions: happy, sad, and nervous. Oh! God can't express it.

My cousins were deciding how much they should ask their brother-in-law for "*joota churai*" with all giggles and laughter. Even I asked them not to back out.

It was 3:30 pm, and my mother came to my room with a cup of chai as we were sipping down the hot cup of chai together. I felt the warmth like never before.

My mother told me, Rukhsar, there is no one like your parents, but it doesn't mean you search for your parents in everyone. Each person has a different way of expressing love. You're going to your in-laws ' house. They'll not pamper you the way we do. Acceptance will take time. She kissed me on my forehead and said may your (*Rukhsar*) dimples never fade away and hugged me tightly.

My tears rolled down my cheeks, although I thought I'd never cry on my D-day. But her hug melted me, and her words touched my heart like an evening star. I needed this. I felt good after those hugs and tears.

Everyone is getting ready as they all need to rush to a wedding venue. It's already time, and we're getting late. My father was shouting how much time will you all take baraat will arrive by then. Hurry up!

Chaos was at its peak. Hahaha! Running, papa getting angry, beautician calling, mummy, be like don't forget to keep safety pins don't ask me later.

At last, we reached our venue on time at 7:00 pm. Soon I got into my room and waited for the baraat to arrive. All my friends were in my room. We had laughter and fun together while eating starter *chicken tikka, french fries, coca-cola, and kababs.*

My friend was teasing me with the name amalgamation of Shayan and Rukhsar #Rukhyan; lol it was embarrassing. Soon we heard the firecrackers, and a big smile was on my face. Yes, the baraat had arrived, and the adrenaline rush in me was unimpressed.

As soon as the baraat came, so did my "*Nikah joda*." It was red and "*Golden gharara with zari work on a georgette dupatta*." I was getting ready for my Nikah Little did I know that something was coming up on my way.

As I was all set to walk down the aisle. My mother came to me, and I asked Ammi where Abba was. I'll walk the aisle with him. My mom was quiet, but I could sense something bad.

I asked my mom what happened, and she said we've cancelled this Nikah. I was shocked and numbed. I got angry with my mom as it was my dream to marry the love of my life.

There was a rage in my eyes against my parents. How can they do this to me? I walked down to my father and asked Abbu what wrong we had done. Please don't do this to me.

My father stood up and hugged me tightly. He said I could let you marry Shayan, but he doesn't deserve you. I asked why.

He said a person who can demand his favourite car at the end of the day could ask for his many favourite things after the wedding. And you're my precious one. If he doesn't value your love, he can't appreciate anything in life. It's not that I can't give him this; it's just that I can't push my daughter into the grave with my own hands.

It shook my world. I looked at Shayan's face and couldn't find that love in his eyes. I felt the betrayal. But I felt strong because of my parents' brave decision of not letting me marry someone whose motive is not to love but greed.

The moment was still. I went back to the room, changed my clothes, came back and returned each thing in front of everyone that belonged to Shayan and asked him to leave with the hope of never seeing each other again.

I was broken inside but was happy that my parents came as a rescue team and saved me from the uncertainties.

I realized that day that nothing lasts forever; I faced my fear of losing Shayan so can you.

Dowry, in the name of gifts, is like covering your grey hair with fashionable colours. Remember, it washes away one day.

I'm happier than before. I got engaged to someone I met six months back at my workplace. I told you nothing lasts forever. I will meet you again. He is waiting for me. We're going on a dinner date. Bye!

Moral of the story

Hello Friends, now you've read my daughter Rukhsar's tory, I would like to have a word with you. I am Rukhsar's Abbu:

I am not an author, I do not know how to dive deep in conversations to bring the pearls of wisdom out. I wanted however to stop you for a while to talk to you as Rukhsar's father who called off his daughter's wedding on the day which was supposed to be the best day of her life. **I did not think, Log kya kahenge as 'Kuch toh log kahenge, logo ka kaam hai kehna'**. (What will people say? People will say something as that's what they do). I did it not because I could not afford to fulfil all those demands but because dowry is disgraceful for our society and we should be ashamed of this culture- both for giving it and for demanding it.

Dowry which historically was a way of giving daughter's share in father's ancestral property at the time of her wedding as gifts has now become a metaphor for an organised crime because of which so many murders and suicides have happened. Leave along those innocent souls who lost their lives, there are so many who are mentally tortured daily and living with a compromised self-respect and dignity (off-course without peace and love too!)

Dowry dehumanises the women, discriminate against the disabled, drown poor parents into further debt, promote dominance of in laws and husbands over women's emotional independence, make child marriages more likely, keep away girls from going to school and have a normal childhood, result in gender inequality and lead to Infanticide.

Remember, dowry makes women a second-class citizen which should not be promoted in 21st century.

I love my daughter and to give her equal rights as her brother, she will get her share in our ancestral property but I will not give any dowry to compensate for this share. I am FEARLESS to say 'NO TO DOWRY'. Join me to do the same and let's change the society together. Few pointers if you want to join me on this path to make this world a better place not only for your daughter for each and every daughter:

- If it's a love marriage, tell you daughter to discuss it with the prospective groom and clarify it that it will be a NO DOWRY ALLIANCE. It is better to end that relationship if there is no agreement to this effect.

- For arranged marriages, discuss this as an initial topic with the groom and his family.

- If dowry demand initiates during the wedding ceremonies, CALL OUT THAT WEDDING. Do not negotiate as this is just the beginning of their endless demands resulting in the lifetime ordeal of your daughter and yourself.

- If demand is made after the wedding, BRING YOUR DAUGHTER BACK IMMEDIATELY, STAND UP NOT ONLY FOR HER BUT FOR YOURSELF AS WELL. Inform immediately to the police of the demand and remember, a single demand is enough to register a case.

- Last but not the least, make your daughter worthy so you do not have to pay someone to marry her. Marriage should be out of love, no alliance for any other reason will result in a happy married life for your Princess. Spend that dowry money to educate her, to set up her business if that's what she wants to do, to send her abroad for higher education. Give her wings to fly not dowry to potential in laws to crucify her and her happiness.

Rukhsar's story from the perspective of our home Poet

It was the day,
The wedding day,
An auspicious day,
Every girl waits,
For this day,
I was no odd,
I waited too,
For this day,
For this day.

Wearing a red Gharara,
Embroidered with,
The strings of gold,
A georgette Dupatta,
The colour is gold,
The nose pin,
Made up of gold,
All the ornaments,
Of the gold,
As all brides do,
With kohl in the eyes,
To avoid the evil eyes,
I was waiting for,
The groom of my life.

I was fallen, in the love of my life,
I had spent, sleepless nights,
With the love, the love of my life,
Texting him, talking to him,
Falling in love, every time,
I talk to him, I talk to him.
My love was the groom,
The love of my life.

I was fascinated, I was excited,
I was curious, I was heated,
For the night of my life,
For that night,
For the wedding night.

I was flying,
The liner of my dreams,
I was in a delusion,
I came out of,
Of this delusion,

When my mother came.

My mother came,
With the tears, she came,
With news, she came,
I asked her about,
With the matter, she came.

She told me a thing,
I was shocked by the thing,
I wanted to cry,
But I couldn't cry,
I wanted to yell,
But I couldn't yell,
I wanted to scream,
But I couldn't scream,
My marriage was broken,
My dreams were broken.

I just didn't believe my ears,
I went to my Dad,
With the bleeding ears,
With the eyes in tears,
Querying him for the reasons,
Of my bleeding ears,
Of my eyes in tears.

He elucidated to me,
My groom was asking,
Asking for the money,
Asking for the dowery.
He added to it,
He could give,
As he had,
The capacity to give,
The money, the dowry,
The groom had asked,
But they could ask for,
The money more,
The dowry more,
More and more.

My love was there,
Besides my Dad,
I just looked,

Looked in his eyes,
Searching for love,
Love in his eyes,
But I couldn't find,
Love in his eyes.
All I could see,
The materialistic eyes.

Then I decided, I determined.
I concluded, I resolved,
To return the thing,
To reciprocate the things,
Things of omen exchanged,
Exchanged with each other,

Souvenir of love,
Ring of love,
Remembrance of love,
All of the love exchanged,
Exchanged with each other,
Moments of love,
We spent,
Spent with each other.

I couldn't sleep that night,
I had to spend a restless night,
With a drenched, pillow in the night,
One more sleepless night.

I went to the state.
The state of depression,
I had seen,
An unhappy me,
A sad me,
A sorrow in me.

But with time,
It was faded,
It had vanished,
But only a glimpse of it,
Is inside me,
To teach me,
A lesson for me,
Not to possess,
Greed in me.

I've someone, someone who loves,
That someone is, whom I love,
He's special, and masters love,
He understands the meaning of love,
Now going to meet my soul of love,
On a craving date with my love.

CHAPTER 4:

CAGED WINGS

"I raise my voice not so I can shout, but so that those without a voice can be heard. We cannot succeed when half of us are held back."
 # Malala Yousafzai

Snapshot

Nobody will rescue you until you do.

Mahek was a teenage girl, a phase where everyone wanted to look cool and be accepted by a famous school group.

Keeping a cell phone is still a dream of many school-going children, and that's what Mahek did.

Her fault was for carrying the cell phone without being noticed at home. Why? Because her family doesn't allow girls to keep cell phones with them.

In the name of freedom, girls are only allowed to study. It is when Mahek realised that until she wouldn't take a stand for herself and came out of the swamp, nobody would rescue her.

Character Sketch

Character description

Mahek is a determined 24-year-old woman; she is young and fair with a short height and wavy hair.

She is working and completing her studies simultaneously. She is an independent woman full of courage and happiness.

Story

I was in the tenth grade when my school held a Christmas party. Having a cell phone with you was a sign of being a cool kid then. One of my classmates brought his cell phone to school to take pictures. We took so many pictures with that phone. After a few days, my father bought a new phone, and his old phone was kept unused, so I decided to use the spare phone to take that to the school party. My friend shared all of the photos on my spare cell phone.

My father was scrolling through that spare phone one day when he noticed all the pictures. He called me "*Mahek*" and asked me about the pictures. I told him that all my friends were posing for photos, so I even did. He slapped me furiously and told me I would never talk to a boy again. He was upset because there were boys in the picture. My father belongs to a North Indian family, and we lived in Mumbai, but my father still believes that girls should go to school and then come straight home. They cannot have male friends. They cannot talk to boys or be friends with them. He assumed I was dating one of my classmates, so he told my mother that wherever I went, whether it was to school, the park, or tuition, she would accompany me.

That day, I cried so much, wondering why I had to go through all this just because I am a girl. And this wasn't even correct. When I asked my mother the same question, she defended her husband, saying, "You're wrong, and you should listen to him." I haven't spoken to any of my family members for a few days because they all said the same thing: I'm getting out of my parents' hands as if I'm committing some major crime.

Apart from academics, I've always wanted to do things like travel, write, and work, but my father wouldn't let me do any of those things. I used to argue with him about the subjects I wanted to study. He wanted me to study for some government exams so that after passing the exams, I could settle down with marriage. At the time, I realized that if I wanted something, I would have to struggle for it. They cannot have complete control over my life. He controls everything in my life, from my clothes to the people I hang out with.

My brother, on the other hand, has none of these restrictions. He is free to do whatever he wants. I started to stand up for myself and told him that I was interested in the media industry and did not want to take any government exams. He started saying, "*I have granted you permission to study.*" That's the biggest mistake of my life. I wish that I hadn't sent you to school to study and all. After hearing that, I had one clear thought in my mind: being a woman is so difficult in this society; how can my basic fundamental right, the right to education, be dependent on someone who believes that girls' greatest privilege is that they are allowed to go to school? It is my right, and no one can take it from me.

My brother and mother supported me, so I left that house and moved to PG. I started looking for work and eventually found one. Then I decided to pursue a career in the media industry, and I recently finished my bachelor's degree. Now, I am a PR Manager at a media organization and am considering pursuing a master's degree. Even though I've been gone for three years, my relatives and father continue to mock me for everything I've done. But now I'm glad that I'm self-sufficient and don't have to rely on anyone for anything.

Sometimes I wonder what my life would be like if I hadn't made the decision to leave the house that day. I suppose I would have married and become reliant on my husband for everything. Now, things are different. Sometimes we have to make tough decisions for ourselves. Being a woman does not imply that you must obey and listen to others all the times. You can accomplish anything you set your mind to; Never give up on your dreams; they are yours, and no one can deprive you of them!

Moral of the story

Gender inequality and discrimination have effects on the girls and those effects are global and somehow lifelong too. This discrimination denies them the basic human rights like education, happy childhood, income equality, a happy married life, peaceful family life and a contended motherhood.

Women usually have less/ no say whether they should be going to school, which subjects they should study, they have no control over what they should pursue as their career and if they should continue with their profession after marriage.

Apart from having the strict rules as to what should we wear, till what time we play in the evening, whether we should go out with our friends for a day out, what and how to talk, how should we walk to the rules are set as to with whom we should talk or indeed with whom we should not talk. Do not laugh out loud, why? Why should someone be able to control the way we live?

We should not go out during our periods, what if they will know that we are on the periods, so what? Isn't it normal to have the periods on a monthly basis for a woman?

Why some girls need to cook dinners at home instead of playing out with the other kids of their age or why do they have to take care of younger siblings instead of doing homework?

Why women have to settle for less? Why can't we have it all? Education, Work, Husband, Children- these are the basics, right? We want all of these as a package deal along with being happy and in love, is it too much to ask? Why do we have to choose?

Giving education to girls is not freedom, it's a fundamental right.

Effects

- Lack of education

- Child marriage

- Exposure to violence

- Objectification of women

- Negative work environment at work places practicing discrimination

- Hinder productivity

- Lack of motivation- conflict between the siblings and at work, between the colleagues

- Anxiety

- Depression

- Patriarchal mindset

We are not asking for more, we are just asking for the equal rights which we deserve as a human being.

As per the former 1st Lady of the USA, Michelle Obama
"No country can every truly flourish if it stifles the potential of its women and deprives itself of the contribution of half its citizens."

"How important it is for us to recognize and celebrate our heroes and she-roes!"
— Maya Angelou

CHAPTER 5:

SHE SURVIVED

Safety and security don't just happen, they are the result of collective consensus and public investment. We owe our children, the most vulnerable citizens in our society, a life free of violence and fear."
#Nelson Mandela. Former President of South Africa

<u>Snapshot</u>

Every cloud has a silver lining.

When Anokhi's laugh was silent by the noise of the belt, her childhood was ruined like a pothole mess.

She lost all her hopes of being happy again, and her parents were waiting for her at the gate.

With each passing day, that little girl was trying hard to overcome her fear when an angel saw her dry tear.

Character's sketch

Character's description

Anokhi is in her late twenties, a girl whose childhood was gloomy but later developed her strong character, and she is a public speaker for NGO now.

Anokhi is dusky with shoulder-length black hair with brown eyes and has a charm in her talking style.

Story

The chirping of children's laughter was louder than the chirping of birds in the evening of Santrampur. Children run freely in this small village in Rajasthan when the Sun starts setting in because there is no more unbearable heat, just the mellow Sun setting slowly while the birds head back to their nests. Some are running around playing with a piece of the old tyre, while some are sitting and playing with their dolls.

Anokhi was one of those who were running after the tyre; she loved to run around; once, she even admitted to her Master Ji in school that she wanted to be like PT Usha. She was a small girl of ten years; she had dark skin and eyes filled with the pure innocence of a child; it was a bliss to watch her talk because she was so passionate about things.

"Anokhi, beta, let's go back home; I have to make roti for your father; he must be on his way back from the town."

Anokhi's father, Kishor was a milkman; he used to milk his own three cows and then sell that milk in the town nearby, while her mother used to stay at home with her. Then Anokhi and her mother, Kamala, headed for home. When her father returned from the deliveries, he greeted his daughter with a pleasant smile and asked her to tell him stories about her day.

From the outside, their family was happy, but one thing that always worried Kishor was his daughter's education. He wanted her to have the best of the best, but they had limited resources. That night Anokhi was sleeping in the room when she heard Kamala crying in the kitchen. She got up and hid behind the door to listen.

"But I don't want my baby girl to go away," Kamala said, sobbing.

"Get a hold of yourself, even though I don't want to live apart from her. This is for her own good. I want my Anokhi to be like PT Usha or anything she wants. But she can't do it in Santrampur." Kishor comforted her.

Kishor was friends with Shukla, who had a friend named Sourabh who lived in Jaipur. Sourabh and his wife Kiran wanted to sponsor a child because they did not have any of their own. They heard of Anokhi and her potential from Shukla and asked if they could sponsor her education in Jaipur. She would have to live with them in Jaipur.

Even though her parents did not want to send their precious child away, they made up their minds and talked to Anokhi about the situation. She was a child who was mature for her age, so she understood and was set to leave.

A few days later, Shukla arrived at their doorstep in his second-hand Wagon R car and loaded up all of Anokhi's luggage and asked Kishor to stay back; he said, "I'll take care of your daughter like she is my own," and they believed him. Kamala cried a lot, and so did Kishor but their Anokhi was brave. She set off on the adventure without shedding tears.

On the way to Sourabh's home, she fell asleep; she did not see the trees on the highway or anything else; she slept the whole time. When she woke up she saw the car was parked in front of a big white and pink house; it seemed to have a small garden with an old car parked beside it. When she entered the house, she saw Sourabh and Kiran waiting for her at their door, they did not smile, but they also did not look unhappy.

Anokhi entered the house, and after a few greetings and introduction Shukla left; they fed Anokhi with good food and let her sleep in a tiny room that had a lot of off-season boxes in it; it was a storeroom. Anokhi did not know what room it was; she was just fine sleeping anywhere. The routine for a few days remained the same Sourabh used to leave for work and come back angry and slam the door while Kiran smoked on the sofa.

A week had gone by, and Anokhi was now starting to question, *"When will I go to school? When can I talk to Baba and Amma?"*

It started to irritate Sourabh, so on the eighth day, he told her, "Get *ready early morning tomorrow.*" Anokhi was happy she thought to herself, *"finally."*

The next day Anokhi got in the car with Sourabh, and they drove off. When they reached the destination, it was just another house; Sourabh introduced her to the house owner, but she never knew their name. She was asked to call him "*Sahab.*" Soon Sahab's wife asked Anokhi if she could cook, clean, and do other household chores and told her to do them nicely while she was there.

It hit her; it was not school; she was never set off to school. But she could do nothing; when Sourabh and Anokhi drove back home, she started questioning him, *"That was not school; I will not have to go there, right? Can you please send me back to my parents?"* Then that little girl started throwing tantrums and crying, which made Sourabh angry. He shouted at Anokhi, and she shouted right back. Soon they were at his home; she dragged her across the living room to the storeroom.

Kiran ran after asking what's the matter. Sourabh told her, "You *stay here; I will handle this girl,*" he shut the door and started slapping Anokhi; when she still did not shut her mouth, Sourabh did the most vicious thing he could. He started to unbuckle his belt and tore her clothes off. He silenced that child's innocence in a way she could never have imagined. She let out silent screams calling out for Kiran, but Kiran knew what her husband was capable of, and she just did not want to be the victim as well.

That was the last day; Anokhi had smiled. She was really silenced. From the next day onwards, Sourabh started to drop her off at his friend's house, where she was supposed to do chores; then, she was picked by Kiran, who then used to make her do all their household chores as well. That little child was suffering in a way no one could imagine in their worst nightmare. She was beaten, abused, forced into labour, and raped multiple times. It was bad; she had bruises all over her body, her private parts used to pain, and she was not really herself anymore.

This went on for months; Anokhi dreamt for a few weeks that her father would beat down Sourabh and rescue her from here. After a while, no one showed up for her, and she had lost all hope. One day, Kiran had a headache, and there was no medicine at home, so she sent Anokhi to the nearby medical shop. She was wearing an old loose kurta, and her hair was loosely tied; she looked like she didn't eat anything for days. Noor, a core team member of Kalyan NGO, was there too. She was visiting the neighbourhood to check out a location for an event next week. She was in the medical shop as well to purchase a few things.

As Anokhi was paying for the medicine, her loose kurta hanging over her fragile body slipped from her shoulder, and that is where Noor comes into play. She saw what horrible bruising she saw on her shoulder; everyone in the shop saw. It was only Noor who had the courage to do something about it. When Anokhi started to walk back home, Noor followed her to Sourabh and Kiran's house.

That is where the rescue for Anokhi started. Noor hung around the house for long hours; she followed them around, and even though she knew she was doing something illegal by stalking them, she knew it was for saving that child. Noor clicked a few photographs of Sourabh dragging Anokhi out of the car and Kiran throwing her in the Sun for hours for not obeying. Noor registered an FIR and involved her NGO in this whole matter.

One fine day, when Noor and the police had everything in place, she knocked on Sourabh's door and asked for Anokhi. When Sourabh got defensive, they broke into his house and saw Anokhi, bleeding from her mouth in a compromised situation; she was barely conscious.

Anokhi was rescued from that hell hole. Kalyan NGO and Noor saved that girl's life. Sourabh and Kiran were charged with Child Labour, Human Trafficking, and Sexually Harassing a Minor repeatedly. While Shukla was charged with Human Trafficking and Child Labour, Anokhi was returned to her parents. They had not lost their hopes in the past few months to see their daughter again; they contacted the police but had no luck finding her.

Noor and Kalyan NGO sponsored Anokhi's education from there on. And when she grew up, she completed her Bachelor's and was now on stage as Gold Medallist receiving her Master's degree in Gender Studies. As twenty-six-year-old Anokhi walks on the stage and stands in front of the microphone, she looks over. The auditorium is filled with her classmates and their parents. Her Baba and Amma were in the front row too. She told her life story out loud for the first time; she was brave. Anokhi had turned her life over; she started from the beginning and was now set to join Kalyan.

Moral of the story

CHILD LABOUR: Not every child working is classified as a child labour. Child labour happens when a child is put to work compromising with their physical and mental health, and education, depriving them of their childhood and a happy family life.

Causes
- Poverty

- Low aspiration

- Huge demand for unskilled and cheap labour

- Lack of education

- Child marriages

- Expensive education facilities

Effects
- Depression

- Social anxiety

- Loss of childhood

- Malnutrition

- Sleeping disorders

- Eating disorders

- Low self esteem

- Self-harm tendencies

- Poverty

Solutions
- Access to free education facilities

- Spread awareness among the employers that it is illegal and immoral to employ child labour.

- Promote fair trade products

- Raise awareness among the parents of the long-term benefits of sending children to school rather than making their child work as cheap labour.

- Financial support to poor families and involving them in Government projects so as to produce stable income for these families.

- Monitoring school attendance and providing support in case of issues.

- Provision of vocational training to the parents

LET'S CREATE AN AWARENESS AND ERADICATE CHILD LABOUR AS IT IS A SOCIAL CRIME. LET'S MAKE IT OUR FIGHT TO WIN IT TOGETHER TO SAVE OUR CHILDREN!!!

As per Rabindranath Tagore, '' Every child comes with the message that God is not yet discouraged of man''. Lets not mistreat them for God's sake as they are the little gifts

CHAPTER 6:

FREE TO FLY

"You're not a victim for sharing your story. You are a survivor setting the world on fire with your truth. And you never know who needs your light, your warmth, and raging courage." — Alex Elle

<u>Snapshot</u>

She found her inner peace.

Marriage is not the ultimate settlement. It's just a requirement of physical and emotional needs, but when you don't get any of these, you start losing hope and feel the disguises.

The same happened with Vidhya, a young girl who married someone who didn't value her presence and abused her.

She didn't reply or walk out of that relationship, but deep inside she always wanted to.

Toxicity in any form is unacceptable, and you should never settle for that.

Character's sketch

Character Description

Vidhya, now 28 years old, mom, daughter-in-law, widow and now the sole earner of the family; husband dies, has to move to a small 2-room space, has to drop out, decides to go back to college.

She has long black and grey hair running down her waist with a small body build and a wheatish skin tone, dark circles with some fine lines on her face.

Story

Summers in Delhi can be very cruel, sweat dripping down the forehead, Metro trains being overfilled, temperature rising beyond expectations, and fans completely starting to be useless. Thinking about Delhi's summer and how fast life is, Vidhya is deboarding the metro train. *This station is Vishwavidyalaya; doors will open on the right, was announced.*

Vidhya was 27 years old now; she was a woman of small build with long black hair running down her waist and wheatish skin. She always dreaded Delhi and did not seem to fit in there. She was married off as soon as she turned eighteen; that's how things used to be in her family.

"Why did everything change? I was used to the way it was," Vidhya thought to herself.

Then immediately shook herself and remembered that today was her first day going to college to complete what she had started. When she entered the college, Vidhya noticed that the garden beside the main gate was kept well, even though it was not too big. The college building was red and off-white with paint cracking in multiple places; it looked serious and sad.

But it was not sad for Vidhya; she went back to studying to make a better future for herself and her family. When she entered the class, she noticed fans barely moving full circles, benches kept at a safe distance because of the global pandemic, and students introducing themselves because it was their first day.

Then suddenly, everyone got attentive; they started to shuffle in their seats, and one student spoke up and said, *"Good morning, ma'am."* And it dawned upon Vidhya; she smiled weakly and said, *"oh, no, no, I am a student too."* Everyone in that classroom got a little awkward; Vidhya settled in a seat up front. Even though she was 27 years old, the dark circles under her big black eyes, greys in her hair, and even some fine lines on her face told a different age.

Sitting by herself, Vidhya started thinking back on the days from a couple of years ago. As she entered in the dream world, she started to think back. In her imagination, the pressure cooker is going wild as Vidhya calls out to her daughter, *"Komal, Komal, are you ready? The school van is waiting for you downstairs!"*

Komal replies, "I am going."

Just then, Uday enters the room and says, *"first, you go ahead and have a girl, and now you can not control her. Control her or my belt, will."* He says while giving a deadly look to Vidhya and Komal, both one by one.

Uday was Vidhya's husband, the one she was married to at eighteen, and he was twenty-four. Uday did not have a fancy job in Delhi, but he used to put food on the table, and that seemed enough to Vidhya's parents. Her mother had told her that the man she was marrying was *"earning enough"* and would keep her well.

She never told Vidhya that he would abuse her and their child daily. Vidhya and Uday's relationship was never based on the feeling of romance, love or friendship; he wanted her to do her household chores and 'give' him a son. Hence, Vidhya could never fall in love with him, their marriage became an obligation, and within a year, they had Komal.

Her mother-in-law, Rekha, grunted a little when Uday gave her threats while praying but never said anything. She seemed annoyed at her son.

As Vidhya was thinking about her life, she heard the class bell, and like that lecture was over, it was time for them to go home. As she boarded the metro train at 4 pm, she could not for the life of her keep her eyes open. She was sleepy, but when she got home, she also had to teach little kids she had been tutoring for six months.

When she reached home, Vidhya was greeted by the smiling face of her nine-year-old daughter. And just like that, suddenly she was not tired anymore. Her home was a two-room apartment with cracks in the wall, but Vidhya and Komal had worked hard to cover those up with posters and paintings and put-up curtains to make it look better.

As Vidhya hugged her child, she harked back to the time in 2020 when Covid 19 was new, and everything was shut. People were forced to live in close quarters with their families, even when they did not want to. This had a horrible impact on Uday; he went from abusive to toxic and unbearable for his family within a matter of a few weeks. As soon as the lockdown regulations became less strict, he started to go out with his friends for an evening cigarette; if Vidhya ever stopped him, he said horrible things to her, so eventually, she stopped.

In no time, Uday caught the virus, which was fatal for him. His weak lungs could not bear the weight of a deadly Coronavirus and gave up. Uday died in 2020 in a hospital nearby, he and Vidhya were married for eight years. When Uday passed away, Vidhya, Komal, and Rekha were left without any income. The company that Uday used to work for and as a salesman went under, and so did his pension fund. Then they had to move to a smaller place.

Even when Vidhya was grieving the death of her husband, all she thought was how she will take care of her daughter now. Never once was she sad. The family lived on scraps for almost a few months. One day a few months after his death, Vidhya woke up and started to brew herself some tea. That day she heard the birds chirping for the first time in many years. She could not help but feel the freedom boiling inside her.

For a few moments, Vidhya felt horrible for feeling that freedom, but that was not her fault; she had been trapped in a loveless marriage with an abusive man for years, and she never knew what happiness felt like until she heard the silence in her apartment without the screaming abuses of an angry man.

That was the moment when Vidhya decided to start tutoring young students. Later she realized that if she wanted to make a more permanent income out of a teaching job, she needed to apply to a few small schools, all the schools required a college degree, and that's how she started taking B.Ed. classes on a government scholarship.

As she let go of Komal after her long hug, Vidhya smiled freely. She knew that even though she was oppressed all her life, it was a hurt that she would never let her daughter face; she would become capable for Komal and make her capable for herself.

This was not the freedom or life Vidhya wanted, and she knew that a life without a husband would be difficult in this world, but it was non reversible.

As many months passed, Vidhya completed her B.Ed. Last semester, during those two years of studying, she got used to being the oldest one there. When she finally completed the course, she was able to get hired by a school, and she even shaped her young daughter into an incredible person. They shared an amazing bond; Komal succeeded in whatever she picked, and without being constantly bickered, she started to thrive like never before.

Moral of the story

"I used to think the worst thing in life was to end up all alone. It's not. The worst thing in life is ending up with people who make you feel all alone"   *# Robin Williams*

A toxic relationship is any relation where one partner abuses the other partner. This abuse could be emotional, physical, mental or financial. Don't stay in a relation where you don't feel safe. Break the relation which makes you feel humiliated, neglected, harassed and exploited. Start looking for something better the day you get this thought in your mind that you deserve something better as you surely do. It's better to be alone than to get tortured which might make you lose your self-respect. STAND UP FOR YOURSELF!

What to do?

- END IT if you don't see the other party changing their attitude and perspective of how to treat you.

- Take care of yourself!

- Open up yourself to a confidential family member/ friend; you don't have to bear all the pressure on your shoulders.

- Seek counselling and Therapy.

"Relationships are supposed to make you feel good. Relationships are NOT supposed to make you feel bad. Or guilty, insecure, ashamed, paranoid, or hopeless. Good. So, when a relationship makes you feel bad, guilty, insecure, ashamed, paranoid, or hopeless, end it." #Laura Bowers

CHAPTER 7:

SCARS THAT DOESN'T SCARE ME ANYMORE

"He changed my face, not my heart. He threw acid on my face, not on my dreams."
#Laxmi Agarwal

Snapshot

All scars have hidden stories.

What Ajay and Vinod did with her and her father can never be forgotten.

Those scars on her face have still made people curious to know about when & why.

But don't you think asking these questions will keep her pain fresh?

She has learned to live with it; don't sympathize, and be empathetic towards them.

Listen to them when they want to share their part. It'll take time, maybe years, but that's how it works.

She dares to face it alone.

Character Sketch

Character Description

A 27-year-old acid attack survivor, she is a happy face with a strong soul.

A girl full of positivity and a strong will to live a life without any hesitation and whining about life scars.

She has a fair skin tone with one side of her face with acid scars and medium hazel colour hair. She has an athletic body with a beautiful smile.

Story

I was 16 at that time, the eldest among my four siblings. The happy and cheerful teenage girl. Reading travelling books and learning about different cultures has always interested me.

I remember it was *"Rabi season"*, and I was sowing *"Sarso"* mustard crop with my father. We were chit-chatting and laughing together.

I was discussing my dreams with baba that one day I'll become a great cook as different cuisines worldwide always inspired me.

Baba said, *"Why not? I'll help all my kids to achieve their dreams"*.

This brings a big smile to my face.

What did I know? My happiness is just for a moment.

The time was around 7 in the morning. I saw two men coming towards us; I told Baba. "Look, Baba, I guess these people are in some need; we should help them."

They came and threw a bottle of acid on my father as we were sitting together. My half face and right hand got affected by the acid attack.

I was screaming and crying with pain Aaaaaaa! Please help me! Help my baba. I felt like I'm in a cage of fire.

Everything was burning. Could hear the cry of baba. He was saying it's painful, it's burning. Pani dalo koi. (someone pour water on us!)

Soon after that, villagers gathered, and I lost consciousness. But I could hear some voices of the bystanders. " Arre kya halat kardi ladki ki, iska marr jaana hi ab theek hai" (her life is now devastated, it's better she should die) and then all blank.

After three days, I woke up in the hospital. Doctors told me I'd lost vision, and some grafting could improve my face. I wasn't yet aware of my appearance.

I asked how baba was. Doctors said he is critical, his face and hands are severely burned. I became quiet, and my heart was crying.

Baba passed away after 15 days. I was still hospitalised and couldn't attend his funeral. After two months, I got discharged. I was happy to go home with Amma, but the home was empty without Baba. I could hear his laughter and the flashbacks of happy memories. I cried my heart out. Felt the emptiness that can never be filled again.

After a week, I went into Amma's room, and I saw amma had masked the mirror with the newspaper.

I removed the newspaper and saw myself for the first time after the attack. I screamed and started crying. My sister (*Mansi*) came running into the room and covered the mirror with her dupatta.

She hugged me tightly and comforted me. Soon my Amma came. Her eyes were filled with tears. She said you're still pretty for me.

I asked Amma why did they attack us? Why only it was me and baba?

Amma then told me those two men (Ajay and Vinod) wanted our land. They've earlier threatened your baba, but he refused to give his hard-earned land to anyone for free or illegally. So they took revenge on your baba by throwing acid on you both.

That day I realised I needed to fight back for my baba's rights. It's time to achieve all the failures and face the truth.

Let the world speak about my appearance. I don't care. Nobody stood with my baba and me when the attack happened. Why should I listen to the world?

The next day I stepped out of my house with courage without covering my face. My siblings and Amma were there with me for moral support.

I heard people whispering look at her, *"Hey! Did you see her scars"? How dreadful she is looking. "Upar wala bachaye sabko" (May God save everyone).* I saw one woman covering her kid's face with her hands so he would not get scared by me.

These things were hurtful in the beginning. I came home, and I cried, but eventually, with each passing day, I became strong and decided to work hard to get those two people behind bars.

I complained about them at the nearest police station. The process was long. Being the eldest, it was now my duty to feed my family as our savings were exhausted in my treatment.

I started my food stall of Aloo paratha with butter on it, served with our special homemade mango pickle and curd. In the beginning, customers were scared to come near my stall.

I got my first customer after a week. They were the school kids. That feeling was excellent, and then there was no stopping again.

Court trials were started. Ajay and Vinod family used to harass me. But these things made me even stronger. I told them now these scars don't scare me anymore. I'll fight for my rights.

They got ten years imprisonment. That day I cried over my victory and felt a sense of happiness. This process took almost two years. I got my land back. It has been seven years now, and I smile freely.

I graduated last year, and my siblings are completing their education. Rajesh and Vyom now look after the land, and Amma and Mansi look after the house.

I've rented a small place where I run a small coffee shop. I always wanted this, and now I'm living it. My siblings helped me during the rush hours. It is how we're intact again.

I do small campaigns and volunteer activities on acid attacks every weekend at my coffee shop and in nearby villages to educate people about the loss one has to face due to these attacks and how you can overcome them.

Again, it's the rabi season, and we're sowing *"Barley"* crops this time. I'll add organic barley water to my menu. Good for detoxification. Hope on your next visit you can try barley water.

Don't forget to finish your club sandwich and latte. I need to prepare my next order. Enjoy your meal.

Moral of the story

ACID ATTACK: We must stand collective against this violence.

Reasons
- Lack of education

- Gender inequality with women considered as a sex object

- Caste and cultural differences

- Lack of awareness in certain sections of society

- Unregulated sale of acid in shops making the predators buy it cheaply to prey their victims. It is available for sale over the counter.

- Hatred to an extent where the predator does not want their victim to die but to disfigure their face leading to social isolation.

What can be done to eradicate this hideous crime?
- Educate young children to respect both the genders and preach gender equality

- National Governments should be hold responsible for framing and implementing laws against acid attacks.

- Victims: although it is very hard for them to face the life normally, it is crucial that they:

    · Must not hide away

    · Do not live in shame or fear

    · Come out and show them they might have burnt your face and body but they could not disfigure your courage.

- Society:

    · Do not limit victim's ability to engage in public life.

    · Do make their fun or talk behind their backs

    · Treat them well and humanly and do not look at them in disgust.

    · WE DON'T ONLY NEED TO HELP VICTIMS AFTER AN ATTACK BUT WE NEED TO TAKE EFFORTS TO CHANGE THE MINDSETS towards unrealistic societal beauty standards.

    · Regulate the sale of acid which will enable the easier prosecution of this inhumane crime (Campaign run by an acid attack survivor, Laxmi Aggarwal).

There are different organisations working to support the Acid attack survivors and their families:

- www.actionaid.org.uk

- www.asti.org.uk

- www.rejuvenceclinic.co.uk

- http://meerfoundation.org (India)

- www.girlsnotbrides.org ACID SURVIVORS FOUNDATION, ASF (Pakistan)

- www.chhanv.org (India)

LET'S TRY AND FIND THE LIGHT AT THE END OF THE TUNNEL BY NOT JUST SURVIVING BUT BY THRIVING!

CHAPTER 8:

MY JOURNEY FROM RAILWAY STATION TO KAMATHIPURA

"All failures - neurotics, psychotics, criminals, drunkards, problem children, suicides, perverts, and prostitutes - are failures because they are lacking in social interest."
— *Alfred Adler*

Chapter Snapshot

Don't trust anyone; people are still relying on and trusting their relatives or acquaintances and sending their young kids to big cities to get rid of their poverty.

Zoya was one of them. She spent half her life in a brothel; not all prostitutes are lucky enough to escape from there, but she made it.

Still, her memories and pains are not yet blurred, but she is happy now with her present life.

Sometimes escaping is the only option to be happy.

Character Sketch

Character Description

Zoya, now in her late 40s, is fair with curly grey and black hair and wrinkles on her face.

She loves wearing sarees and weaving sweaters for her livelihood. Zoya is cheerful and helps others without any questions.

She still has those dark memories, but she doesn't let them overshadow her happiness.

Story

It was raining heavily—Mumbai, then Bombay. In 1975, a train arrived at *Bombay Central Railway Station*. A 11-year-old girl wearing a red floral frock with patches on it and a jute bag hanging over her shoulder got off the train.

The girl had a gleam in her eyes, a new hope of happiness. Her dry curly hair and dry lips were a testimony to the fact that she was poor.

Unaware of the brutal truth, Zoya was having tea and Parle-G biscuits at the railway station to satisfy her hunger and was excited that Mushtaq Bhai would take her to the workplace.

Then both left from the railway station. A white Ambassador car was waiting for them outside, and as soon as she sat down in the car, Zoya started weaving dreams for her happy life.

She saw such big roads and buildings for the first time. What did anyone know that happiness is only for a few moments?

In an excited tone she asked *"Mushtaq bhai kya wo bade log bhi mujhe aise gaadi mein ghoomayenge"* (*"Mushtaq Bhai, will those big people also drive me in a car"?*)

Mushtaq replied- *"Haan kyun nahi, bas tum kaam achche se karna"*. (*"Yes, why not? Just do the job well"*.)

59

Then the car stopped in a locality, and little Zoya was told to stay in the car until Mushtaq came back.

Sitting by the car window, listening to the people's words, people were standing outside the grimy and cramped buildings, and strange words were said to every passing girl.

Mushtaq Bhai came and took Zoya to one of the brothels in Kamathipura. The entrance of the building looks like a cage with iron rods on the gate. The building walls were cracked.

There was a big hall with a chess pattern floor and blue walls and sofas with one old chandelier. A middle-aged woman was sitting in that hall wearing a "*pink banarasi saree and gold earrings*" and a bindi on her forehead. That hall was a meeting point for Nyka (*Saroj Bai*) with pimps and clients.

There were overdressed women all around. While standing in the room. She heard a woman "*Nyka*" tell some men, "We have got a fresh piece for you" (Naya maal aaya hai market mein bilkul taza).

Zoya said to Mushtaq Bhai, "*I do not want to work here. Take me with you*".

Everyone in the room laughed at Zoya. Mushtaq left the place after taking a handful of money.

Then the auction started at ₹2,000, 5,000, 15,000, and stopped at ₹30,000.

And this is how "*I*", the virgin girl "*Zoya*", was sold for the first time. They took me to get dressed and wear loud makeup like adults. I was crying loud out in fear of what was happening around me.

I was told if I'll not stop crying, they'll beat me to death. I got scared I was a little girl. I was presented in front of the client for the first time.

It was scarier than your imagination. I was running and shouting. The Nyka and guard held my hands and feet, and the client was raping me. I was in blood and pain for 24 hours, and I lost consciousness.

I got hospitalised for 3.5 months. The brothel bore the cost, and since then, I have been in debt. And I was brought back to the brothel to pay off the debt.

They locked me in a dark room naked, without food for 1.5 months and used to beat me with belts and rods. I used to scream, cry and get raped every day.

I was silent for years. Only clients used to come and go. My family thought I was working as a house helper in Bombay.

I felt "I was born in a wrong place, doing the wrong thing". I asked God, Is this my fate? *Zoya said in a cracked voice.*

Many questions were unanswered. What did I know that poverty would bring me here?

It was not easy to escape from the Kamathipura brothel; you'll find guards on each nook of the street.

But I collected each broken piece of mine when I saw an 8-year-old girl Nepali girl was trafficked to the brothel, and I thought I'll not let them ruin her innocence.

I was 25 then. I helped that girl to escape from that hell, but fortunately, she escaped, and I was caught. I was beaten to death. They raped me multiple times to silence me. The mark on my forehead is the memory of the beatings, they kept hitting, and I got stronger.

It must have been some 1:30 in the night. There was a sound of running in the brothel, and my luck was strong that day God had listened to me.

By the grace of God, there was a raid on Brothel in 2006, and it was a golden opportunity in my life. When the police were taking Nyka and the guards in the police car, then my steps did not stop. I took out 4 other sex workers with me, and we ran away from there.

I ran into an NGO, "*Save Savita*", that rescued sex workers.

Those people were angels for me. Abhishek Bhaiya (NGO owner) taught us the art of weaving, cooking, baking and other activities to live our life ahead of our own will.

Today I've collaborated with 5 NGOs that help rescue sex workers and work on their upliftment.

Many sex workers are not able to be rescued, so our NGOs educate and take care of their children so that they do not have a negative effect mentally and emotionally.

The brothel is a nightmare for every girl. I wish even the enemy doesn't go into that swamp. There you will see that the woman pulls you into that flesh market.

It has been 47 years, and no women in Kamathipura came with their own will or were happy with their work.

We're warriors, and Kamathipura is a battlefield. Either you will die yourself, or you will come after killing others.

Moral of the Story

PROSTITUTION is a major social issue and is a crime. A prostitute may be a male, female or a transgender, this is a person who do sexual activity not with their partner or spouse but with strangers for money/ valuables. It is more hideous for women and young girls as no money can break the pain, helplessness and brokenness of a woman who is forced to sleep with a client. NO CONSENT even if the money charged for doing it is still a NO. As per the survey conducted by Street Light UK, when asked if they want to leave the profession, 9 out of 10 women said YES and these results speak volume to justify my point above.

Reasons for entering in this flesh trade

Prostitute life is a choice for some but an obligation and a force for the majority of these sex workers. No one is born a prostitute though there is no single door into this hideous and painful world from where apparently there is no comeback to live a dignified life again.

Some reasons include:

- Homelessness

- Poverty

- Lack of education

- Sexual curiosity

- Unemployment leading to many young girls opting to enter this living hell to earn more money while they are still young.

- Sexual abuse at younger age

- Domestic violence

- Drug addiction

- Debt

- Way to pay for their university fees if the parents cannot afford to pay it for these future bright young women.

Effects

- Post Traumatic Stress Disorder (PTSD)

- Life long effects splitting between body, mind, heart and soul

- Sleeping disorder

- Eating disorder

- Depression

- Anxiety

- Self-harm tendencies

- Drug addiction and mental illness

- Low self esteem and feeling of worthlessness as they are only considered as flesh and a body and not a human being with feelings and emotions

- Panic attacks & Flashbacks

- Violence

- Self-hate

- Sexually transmitted diseases like AIDS

- Unwanted pregnancies and lack of education for the children of the prostitutes leading to poverty and exploitation of these innocent kids.

What can be done to eradicate Prostitution from our society?

- Sex work should be treated as a profession. In India, actually Supreme court gave this ruling recently. Watch out my video on my You tube channel: (https://youtu.be/5pfAw6sNEIA)

- For those who are in this profession as an informed choice and feel safe, they should have the option of remaining in their profession and they should have access to the basic human rights like:

    • Healthcare facilities to avoid sexually transmitted diseases and during the pregnancy and child birth.

    • Knowledge, awareness of and free access to condoms and other contraceptive measures to avoid the spread of STDs and to avoid unwanted pregnancies.

    • Vocational training to help them to learn new skills (knitting, stitching, cooking, baking, IT, beauty etc) so they have the means to earn livelihood so as to make an easy route for them to leave this profession without falling in the pit of poverty and homelessness.

    • Access to good education to their children.

    • Equal status in society, they should be treated as humans with heart and soul and not just the flesh of the woman body.

    • Social networking so they can meet others within and outside this trade so they develop awareness and develop friendships with a motive to have a strong emotional support when in need. WOMEN

OUT OF THE TRADE SHOULD BE TRAINED, MOTIVATED AND SUPPORTED TO COME FORWARD TO HELP WITH THIS INITIATIVE FOR THE BETTERMENT OF THOSE WHO ARE STUCK IN THIS TRADE.

- Forced labour in this trade should have an opportunity to leave and live a NORMAL DIGNIFIED life outside this BROTHEL (which stinks) they're stuck in surrounded by pimps. Society can help these women by building:

  • Shelter homes and Rehabs: to provide safe environment to them post exit and to support them to recover from the trauma and anxiety.

  • Providing Counselling services: to support them again with their mental condition and to show them that this finally the end of the tunnel for them.

  • Good health care facilities, Vocational training and good education to their children, as discussed above.

PROSTITUTION EXISTS AS THERE IS SOMEONE WHO IS WILLING TO PAY MONEY FOR SEX WHICH IS IMMORAL AND UNETHICAL, SEX SHOULD BE OUT OF LOVE AND NOT FOR THE MONEY AND LUST AND TO ERADICATE THIS FROM OUR SOCIETY, WE NEED TO EDUCATE THIS TO OUR CHILDREN AT THE VERY YOUNG AGE THAT SEX SHOULD NOT BE BOUGHT LIKE FRUITS AND VEGETABLES!!!

THIS AWARENESS WILL SAVE MANY INNOCENT LIVES!!!

CHAPTER 9:

IT WAS BITTERSWEET

"No government has the right to tell its citizens when or whom to love. The only queer people are those who don't love anybody. ''   *#Rita Mae Brown*

<u>Snapshot</u>

Sometimes what you see is just what they want you to see.

Arjun could have shared his life before, but the fear of judgment made him wear a mask.

Nobody chose Arjun, but Arjun chose his world of acceptance with no regrets with the help of Reena.

The reality hits Reena at first, but she realizes it is not society. It's his family that made him wear this mask for so long.

Sometimes people die with masks on because the reality is harsh, as we are still in a taboo where a man can only love a woman, not anyone else.

It was difficult for both of them to realise the truth, but in the end, they did what was right for each other.

Homosexuality is not a sin; it's natural. LGBTQ communities should not be targeted or made fun of. What matters the most is humanity above everything else.

Character Sketch

Character description

Reena is 30 now, and she is tall with caramel hair and a wheatish skin tone and dark eyes. She believes in not sticking to a place that doesn't belong to you.

She is a firm believer and now helps her ex-husband, now friend, to raise her voice for the LGBTQ Community.

Story

Reena has always dreamed of her honeymoon in Italy. She wants to stroll the streets of *"Sicily"* and watch the sunset with her love in *"City of Salt and Sail."*

And yes, Arjun fulfilled his wife's dream and took her to Italy after marriage.

Reena couldn't believe she was witnessing her dream as she drank a glass of wine while watching the sunset with Arjun. Reena kissed Arjun on his cheeks and said, *"Thank you."*

They both smiled, and Arjun placed his hand on Reena's shoulder.

Arjun and Reena had so much fun together, from drinking, dancing, snorkelling and laughing. Although it was their honeymoon, Arjun told Reena both should take time to understand each other better.

To which Reena agreed, and they became good friends. Arjun tries to fulfil all her wishes.

Reena, on a call with her mother, "Mummy, I'm so thankful to God for giving a life partner like Arjun. I feel blessed."

Reena's mother replied, "May god protect you from evil eyes, my love."

And a month passes like this.

"It was a cold evening when they both were having a cup of coffee together on their balcony, wearing the same blanket and looking up to the sky."

Reena expressed her feelings to Arjun, *"Hey! Do you know what?"*

Arjun asked, *"What?"*

Reena placed her head on Arjun's shoulder and said, *"I've fallen in love with you."*

Reena was waiting for Arjun's reply.

"There was silence in the air."

Arjun puts his cup of coffee on the table and hugs Reena tightly.

Reena felt that moment as a *"Mediterranean Winter Breeze."*

Arjun whispered in Reena's ear, *"I'm sorry, please forgive me and started crying."*

Reena could not understand anything and said, *"Are you okay?"*

Arjun then said, *"I'm gay."*

"What?" Reena said in a surprised tone.

Reena became quiet for a moment and asked Arun, *"Then why did you marry me?"*

Arjun replied, *"I did not have the courage to tell anyone about my sexual orientation"*.

"I'm scared about the reactions. Please, Reena, don't tell anyone about this."

Reena did not respond to Arjun's words, and she was crying in anger.

She felt betrayed *"like it was raining in the sun."*

Reena did not understand what to do or whom to tell; she did not want to live in this marriage anymore.

A week has passed, and Reena is still in search of answers.

That night Arjun came home, and at the dinner table, he put himself together and confessed his reality to the family.

And suddenly, everyone looked at Arjun's face, shockingly even Reena.

Arjun's father, *"You're a man, my blood; don't forget about your legacy."*

Arjun's mother from the other side of the dinner table, *"Arjun beta, you're my only son; how could you say something like this? You should consult a doctor."*

Arjun's sister, *"Bhaiya, please, what will my friends say; it'll be so embarrassing."*

Arjun replied, *"This is who I'm; this is the real me. I'm gay, and I love someone else.*

And I have decided to divorce Reena. I don't want her to suffer along with me.

Arjun's family got angry.

Arjun's father said angrily, slamming his hand on the table, *"Let's end this conversation here. Nothing should get out of this room. I'll not tolerate such things; this is against our culture."*

Reena was sitting quietly at the table and watching everyone's behaviour.

And everyone went to their rooms.

Arjun also went towards his room.

Reena felt that *"Karma"* was supporting her, and she felt good that Arun was going through this.

As Reena entered the room, she saw Arjun crying. He was crying differently, a cry of fear, judgement and losing loved ones.

Arjun asked Reena, *"Being a man, am I not allowed to choose my partner?"*

"Is being gay a curse or shameful act?"

"I was always scared to face these reactions." Arjun continues sobbing.

Reena did not respond to Arjun's talk and went to sleep.

Reena couldn't sleep the whole night and kept thinking about the situation.

"Should I forgive Arjun?"

"What will society say to me? Her husband is gay.

"No. I can't."

"It'll be a shame for me."

Reena closes her eyes, and she remembers the moments in Italy when Arjun tried to make her every dream come true.

Tears rolled down from Reena's eyes.

Reena realised life is about mistakes and errors, but Arjun is pure and real.

All this time, he was living in a shell of fear.

She decided to stand for Arjun's rights and fought with his family.

They both mutually divorced each other on a good note.

Reena loved Arjun, but she understood letting go of someone you love is the best option.

They're still good friends, and Arjun and Reena are still fighting for his right to be gay.

It's not that society didn't accept him; it's his own family.

Reena and Arjun now run a campaign on LGBTQ rights and culture along with Arjun's gay partner Sagar.

Moral of the story

Sexual orientation is a crucial aspect of a person's identity in relation to their romantic attraction. It includes Gay, Lesbian, Bisexual, Straight or Asexual.

There is a vast difference between Sexual orientation and Sexual Identity and we must not confuse between these terms. Sexual orientation is with whom you want to be associated romantically while Sexual Identity is about who you are.

Only you can/ should decide what sexual identity best describes you and its OK also not to be labelled. YOUR LIFE, YOUR DECISION! This is true with your sexual orientation too, it is a matter of our own personal choice and it should not be infringed with.

Being a gay/ lesbian is not an illness, the same way like being straight is how you are born as, being a gay/ lesbian is what you are born as.

· Do not bully/ torture/ harass them for who they are.

· Do not gossip about them behind their backs and do not make fun of them.

· Do not limit their ability to engage in public life.

· Do not force them to use medicines to cure of something which is not an illness.

· In some European countries/ Africa/ India, Black magic is apparently used to convert their sexual orientation to Straight. No BLACK MAGIC can make this happen, a person is born like that.

· Support your child who is LGBTQ, DO NOT NEGLECT/ ABUSE them. Accept them as a normal child as they are indeed NORMAL. Do not try to make your child's sexual orientation a matter of family honour

CHAPTER 10:

BROKEN BUTTERFLY

"Age does not matter in most relationships, but in marriage, it matters a lot. If you marry a younger you have to baby sit, and if you marry an older, you have to follow orders."
#M.F. Moonzajer, LOVE, HATRED AND MADNESS

<u>Snapshot</u>

When a caterpillar turns into a butterfly, its beauty is enhanced, and they get wings to fly high, but many girls like Rumaisa, who are forced to get married in their teenage years, lose all hopes and happiness.

Child marriages are still existing; a girl who gets married at twelve years and gets pregnant at thirteen while their husbands leave them as they're not useful; can't do household chores properly.

Stop whataboutery.

Why don't you realize child marriage is a trauma for boys and girls both? Such families are not only ruining their child's life physically but emotionally and mentally too.

When a child says no to anything, it means they're not ready for it. You can't force your thoughts on them because *"Rishta achcha aaya hai."* (It's a good alliance)

Let your child fly with coloured wings; don't bury their emotions because you're free from liability.

Character Sketch

Character description

Rumaisa is now 17, a new young mother to a beautiful daughter. She has a petite body built with dry brown curly hair, wears salwar suits, and always covers her hair with a dupatta.

She now works as a housemaid in Kolkata to make a better life alone.

Story

It was December 2018. I took a break from my work and decided to visit Kolkata to explore its popular rich culture that I've seen through books and travel shows.

I landed in Kolkata at 11:00 pm. I was standing at Gate No 1 A, waiting for my cab to arrive.

Soon my cab came, a *Silver Tata Indigo car*, and I got into the cab.

While on my way to the hotel, my cab driver asked, *"Madam aapko kahin bhi Kolkata mein ghoomna ho, mein aapko ghooma dunga."* (*Madam, wherever you want to roam in Kolkata, I will take you around.*)

I said "kitna *charge karoge per day ka?"* (*How much will you charge per day?*)

The cab driver replied, "₹*4500 per day*".

I said, *"okay"*.

Then we both become quiet; he turns his car radio to a medium volume. I could hear a Bengali song playing in the background. The tune was soft and melodious.

I reached my hotel at 11:45 pm and asked the driver to come tomorrow at 4:45 am as I want to see the sunrise at Hooghly River.

I checked into the hotel, freshened up, set the alarm on my mobile and slept.

Alarm rang, and it was already 4:00 am. I did not want to leave my cosy warm bed, but I got up, ordered a cup of Chai with one plate of potato cutlet, took a bath, wore a casual outfit and got ready.

My breakfast came. And I peeped outside the blinds, which were still dark. I checked the temperature outside, and it was 12 degrees. I decided to wear a jacket.

My phone rang exactly at 4:45 am, and it was the driver's call. I picked up his call. He said "madam *mein hotel aagaya hu."* (*Madam, I'm at the hotel.*)

We reached Princep ghat at 5:00 am, and my driver booked a half-hour boat ride for me at ₹300. I took my cab driver along with me on the boat ride. We were three on the boat, all peacefully sitting and living the moment.

I witnessed the beauty of Howrah bridge on one side and Vidyasagar Setu on the other. The sun started rising, and the sky was pale blue and orange.

The birds were chirping; the wind was blowing, the peace was unimpressed, and just a girl sitting on the river bank was crying while looking at the sky.

Curiosity arises in me. Why is this girl crying alone in the morning, looking at the sky? What is the reason?

I told the boatman to take me to the girl sitting on the bank of the river.

My driver then said "*Arre madam aisi kayi kam umar ladkiyan milengi aapko aasman ko dekh kar rote hue.*" (*Ma'am, you will find many such young girls crying looking at the sky.*)

I gave a confused expression! I asked Why? Is it normal in Kolkata for young girls to cry on riverbanks?

My driver said, "*They're all broken butterflies of Malda, and they can't fly anymore*".

This metaphor shook me.

Malda? And soon, the boat came to the bank of the river. The girl was still sitting there glaring at the sky with hope.

The driver and the boatman were sitting in the boat. The driver was taking a picture of the river.

I went to the girl and asked *Hey! Can I sit here*? "*She looked at me and said nothing*".

A tea seller was passing from there; I stopped him and said, "*bhaiya*", give me four tea.

I offered an extra cup of tea to that girl. At first, she refused, but at my request, she took that cup of tea.

While sipping our hot chai from "*Kulhad*", I asked what's your name and how old are you?

She said *"Rumaisa"*, and I'm 16 years old.

Then again a pause in our conversation.

I said "Rumaisa" do you know? When we cry looking at the sky, it's because we don't trust anyone except the Almighty, and that hope keeps us alive.

"Rumaisa started crying and looked at me with too many questions in her eyes".

She then said It had been two years now. I lost all my hopes, dreams and happiness. Since then, I have looked at the sky every day and cried my heart out.

I held her hand, and Rumaisa continued her story. I was 14 years old and a bright, intelligent student.

It was summer. I came home, and my mother told me we'd fixed your marriage and you'll get married by the end of the week.

This news broke me apart. I started crying and begging my parents that I wanted to continue my studies. I don't want to get married. Let me finish my studies, please.

They ignored all my talks. I ran to my friends, who helped in stopping child marriage.

My friend Rehana was 17; then, they played an act in a village area to create awareness about the consequences of child marriage.

My friend, a team leader of that group, is also a victim of child marriage, but she escaped from her marriage and started her own small NGO in an alliance with a local school that rescues young girls and boys from child marriage.

I told them about my wedding date so that they could stop my marriage.

On my wedding day, 03 May 2016, police came and stopped my wedding. I was the happiest on earth, but it didn't last long.

My family made me marry at midnight a man who was 12 years older than me.

Now, I'm three months pregnant. And my husband left me because I was of no use to him. I don't want this to happen with my child, whether a girl or a boy.

I've decided to fight for my child's rights. I'll work as a house-help, so I don't need to beg anyone.

Right now, I'm living with my parents in Malda. I came to Kolkata in search of work.

Child marriages are toxic. You're not treated like a human. Just a machine for pleasure.

Rumaisa, in the end, *"Didi Malda has many broken butterfly stories".*

We then parted ways as my half-hour boat ride was about to end.

Moral of the story

CHILD MARRIAGE is any marriage where at least one of the partners is under 18 years of age.

Reasons

- Gender Inequality

- Language barriers

- Lack of educational opportunities

- Limited access to healthcare

- Reduction of economic burden/ way to earn income

- Belief that it will secure the girls and will protect their future

- Customs and Culture in some sections of the society

Effects

- Girls lose their childhood

- Domestic violence

- Lack of education as this marriage forces the girls to leave the school

- Early and difficult pregnancies

- Worse economic and health conditions than their unmarried peers

- Less strength to stand up for their own kids and their kids get married at an early age too, so this vicious circle continues.

- Isolate young girls from society, no participation in the society, lack of awareness and ruin both their physical and psychological well-being.

What can be done?

- Educate parents and community leaders

- Comprehensive sex education at adolescent age in school

- Monitoring school attendance and providing support in case of issues

- Provision of life skills training to the adolescent girls

- Teach boys to respect the girls, to educate them of gender equality

- Advocate young people to advocate and campaign against child marriage (plan-uk.org)

REMEMBER: A CHILD MARRIAGE IS A VIOLATION OF CHILD RIGHTS AND SHOULD BE PROHBITED.

EMPOWER GIRLS TO HAVE AN EMPOWERED FUTURE!!!

CHAPTER 11 :

STUCK IN THE WEB

''We don't need bigger cars or fancier clothes. We need self-respect, identity, community, love, variety, beauty, challenge and a purpose in living that is greater than material accumulation''.
#Donella Meadows

<u>Snapshot</u>

The realisation of Self-respect.

Niharika had all the luxuries of life after her marriage, but she was losing her self-respect with each passing day.

She was not ready for all that Dev was doing with her, but she was scared to speak up.

Why is walking out of a toxic marriage still not acceptable in India? Niharika was living in a cloud of thoughts of disdain, but a little push by Sarita that has ignited the power in her and to realise if she would not stand for her; none will.

When you feel something is wrong and going through a round of insults directly or indirectly, move out from that place, and leave that person forever immediately.

Nothing is more important than your self-respect.

Character Sketch

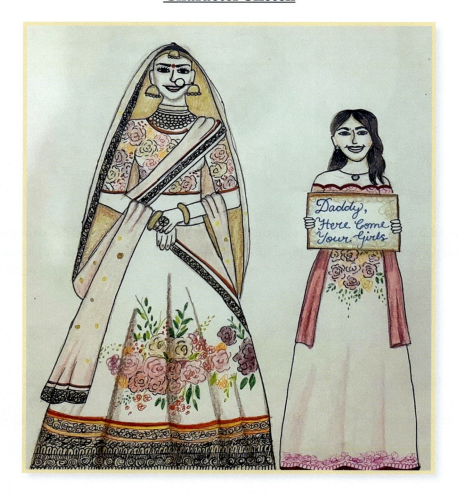

Daddy, Here Come Your Girls

Character Description

Niharika is now 38 years old; she is tall with high cheekbones and beautiful black eyes with long bobs and a perfect smile.

She is a cafe owner in Mumbai and looks after her family.

If beauty has a definition, Niharika is the example.

Story

He grabbed my hair tightly and dragged me to the bedroom; Then, he slapped me and pushed me to the ground. I was crying in pain.

That was the first time that I raised my voice on Dev for cheating on me.

His girlfriend was in the other room. She unheard all my screams.

My maid came into the room; she picked me up from the ground, cleaned my mouth, and gave me a glass of water.

My maid was looking at my face with questions in her eyes; She then unveiled the window to let the sunshine come.

She was quietly standing and looking outside the window, and I was sobbing in pain.

We could hear the laughter from the other room. My maid asked, *"Madam, what's your compulsion that you're still in this marriage?"*

I looked at her and asked, *"What would you do? If this had happened to you?"*

Dev called Sarita, *"Sarita, Serve lunch."*

Sarita then goes and starts preparing the lunch table.

I was sitting alone in the room and looking at the reflection of the sun where I recalled how I've been tolerating this from the first week of my marriage.

I was 20 when I got married to Dev; just after a week of my marriage, I went to the kitchen at midnight to make tea for Dev as he was doing work in his study.

I made tea and went to the study room, and the door there was slightly open when I saw for the first time that Dev was making love with the maid.

I shouted in anger Dev, what are you doing? and slapped the maid.

For how long have you been doing this? Do you people love each other?

Dev laughed at me. Love? Seriously! It's fun, not love. I only love you, Niharika.

"There was such pain in my heart as if someone had pricked the thorns of a rose."

Before I could ask him anything again, he said in a loud voice, "Look, *I'm giving you good food, shelter, and fancy clothes. You should be thankful to me."*

His behaviour was shocking to me.

And then, after four months, I became pregnant, and Dev started bringing prostitutes home.

This was his routine behaviour and lifestyle. And I couldn't resist this, so I raised my voice five months after our wedding because I didn't want my child to be born in this atmosphere.

I was scared to raise my child with Dev. When I was getting married, people blessed me to have a beautiful life, but I was living in hell.

I was scared to tell my parents as getting divorced 20 years back was not an easy thing.

But when Sarita asked me about my compulsion that day and I was staring at the reflection of the sunshine. I realized, *"Why am I still here?"*

I'm free; I'm not bound to live in this toxic relationship. I don't need anyone's opinion to leave Dev.

I wiped my tears that day, and it was forever. I chose to step out of the web, packed my bags, and left the house with no regrets.

When I was leaving the house and passed by the living area where Dev was sitting with one of his girlfriends, he stopped me and said, *"You will regret Niharika; I know you'll come back within a week. Where will you get this lavish life?"*

I replied, *"I can make my life lavish; you make yourself human first."*

I never looked back after that. We divorced each other. I gave birth to my beautiful daughter *"Mallika."* My parents were the support system throughout my journey, and I started my book store in Mumbai with a café theme. My cafe earned popularity within no time.

I don't know where he is now. But I'll always be thankful to Sarita. Her question has ignited the power in me of my self-respect and confidence, which I was losing with Dev.

This year I'll be 37, and I've fallen in love again with a man who loves me, respects my dignity, and cares for my daughter. Abhijeet and I are getting married next month. My daughter Mallika is excited; so am I.

Moral of the story

Self-respect is having pride and confidence in oneself, loving oneself above and beyond and is a trait to treat ourselves with honour and dignity.

DO NOT LET YOURSELF BE SOMEONE ELSE'S PUNCHBAG. Always admire yourself of how you look (your physical appearance), who you're as an individual, what you're capable of and what you can achieve. As a human being, being respected is your basic human right and you SHOULD respect yourself too. If you respect yourself, you're telling others to respect you too. So, set the correct standards!

You're the most important in your life and you need to take care of yourself before anyone or anything else.

Ways to achieve Self respect

- Set the firm boundaries for others as to what is acceptable to you and what will not be tolerated when they deal with yourself.

- Yoga and meditation help in relaxing mind and think calmly and hence achieving self- respect.

- Say 'No' more often. Feel under no compulsion to say 'Yes' for anything which makes you uncomfortable.

- Live your life on your terms, grow with life to achieve a new height, do not be stagnant and be your own hero. You might lose some relations in the process but that's life, not everyone came in our lives to stay forever.

- Do not get overwhelmed easily, learn to manage and control your emotions as self-respect cannot be practised until your emotions are managed well.

- Do the RIGHT THING even if you're the only one doing it.

- Do what makes you feel HAPPY & CONTENDED, others don't have to like it and you don't have to really care.

- STAND UP FOR YOURSELF and YOUR DECISIONS. Be willing to be flexible to learn and adapt but NEVER COMPROMISE YOURSELF to fit in with a particular person or a situation. YOU DON'T HAVE TO TOLERATE DISRESPECT and make it very clear to others.

- BE YOU & ONLY YOU, authentic 'YOU'. Never lose yourself, your identity in the process of 'fitting in'.

- Choose HONESTY always. Be honest with yourself as a starting point. It could be hard to tell the truth but truth should always prevail.

- YOU CAN CHANGE ANYTIME, DO NOT FEEL THE PRSSSURE OF STICKING TO AN OLDER VERSION OF YOU, NOT NEEDED.

> *"This is not just about women. We men need to recognize the part we play, too. Real men treat women with the dignity and respect they deserve."* **#Prince Harry**

"Each time a woman stands up for herself, she stands up for all women."

#Maya Angelou

CHAPTER 12:

GOWN OF PRIDE

"I didn't plan on being a single mom, but you have to deal with the cards you are dealt the best way you can."
#Tichina Arnold

<u>Snapshot</u>

Making decisions at the right time is crucial, but they're fruitful in the end.

This is what Advocate Rohima did. She could have cried for the loss of her husband's demise, but she chose to be strong and utilise her education to make a better living for herself and her daughter.

It wasn't easy for her to move out with a year-old daughter to a new city, but she did it, and now she is making each moment memorable with her daughter.

Advocate Rohima is an example of how single parents can make their decisions alone by reducing dependency on others.

So crying is just an excuse to fight the obstacles and time.

Character Sketch

Character's description

Rohima is 32 years old now; she is the definition of a powerful woman. A tall woman with black curly shoulder-length hair with a middle parting and a fair skin tone.

Rohima is currently a practising lawyer in Sivasagar, Assam. She has chosen education and happiness and made herself independent.

Story

We met for the first time at our maternal aunt's place. It was a dinner party.

I didn't know that this meeting of the eyes for a few moments would become life for both of us.

That's how Mustak and I met and became friends.

My school was completed. I planned to study Law at the *Bangalore Institute of Legal Studies.*

At the age of 19, I left *Sivasagar, Assam* (my hometown), and boarded the steps toward my dreams of becoming a lawyer.

Within no time, I got a surprise. Mustak came to Bangalore, too, for his *Animation studies.*

And our bond became much more potent than before. We dated for eight years.

After completing my LL.M, I came back to Assam.

I wanted to talk to my mother about Mustak, but I was nervous about her reaction.

But we both gathered the courage and talked to our families about our relationship.

They said, "Yes."

"Isn't it a fairy-tale?" I said to Mustak on the phone.

Mustak replied, "It's all destiny, and we're destined to be together."

Our happiness has no boundaries.

Life was giving me everything that I asked for.

Soon the day arrived, and we got married on 4th June, 2015.

Everything seems like *"Springtime."*

I conceived in 2017; Mustak was the happiest on earth. He started weaving dreams of his fatherhood.

"We will do this with our child; we'll make them do whatever they want. I'll work hard for my child's better future."

It was September 25th, 2018. Our daughter was born. Mustak held our daughter in his arms and named her Amayra.

We thanked the Almighty together for this beautiful life.

I was at my parents' house. Amayra was only 40 days old.

My phone rings.

Mustak, "Rohima, I'm diagnosed with oral cancer."

I replied, "Everything will be fine. You'll be healed soon."

I was a new mother, too exhausted to feel the situation, but I had a hope that with advanced treatments, Mustak would become healthy again.

My In-laws took him to Chennai for an operation, which was successful.

We become happy again.

Little did I know that my happiness was like the *"Winter Sunshine."*

But Mustak's health was not recovering, so we thought of revisiting a doctor.

It was March 2019 when Amayra was six months old, and we went to Chennai for the diagnosis and then to Mumbai.

I was carrying Amayra when the doctor called me and told me that Mustak had been diagnosed with Metastasis and he had only *"3 months left to live"*.

"This news shook me to the bones. I felt completely shattered, helpless. time stopped for me".

Mustak passed away on 23rd September 2019, two days before Amayra's first birthday.

Before he died, Mustak prepared everything for his daughter's first birthday. He was excited, ordered the cake, and made arrangements for the birthday party.

But God has his own plans, and Mustak couldn't survive till our daughter's first birthday.

But I held myself tight and strong and celebrated Amayra's birthday in my room with other kids because this is what Mustak wanted.

After my husband's death, I started facing monetary issues, and our savings were exhausted.

I looked at my daughter's face and realized she was my motive to live again.

I decided to leave home ten days after Mustak's demise and go to Guwahati, where I could work out of memories and build my daughter's future.

I decided to move out with my daughter, and I stood firm and started practicing as a lawyer in 2019 at *BDK Law Associates, Guwahati.*

It was Pandemic 2021 when my mother asked me to return to Sivasagar and do my work there.

I thought about it and moved back to my maternal house, where I opened my chamber and became an *Advocate Rohima Mustak* who is now a practicing lawyer at *Sivasagar Bar Association* and recently appointed as *Panel Advocate of ONGCL Sivasagar.*

Now I'm the father and mother both. I've decided to wear my *"Gown of Pride"* because nobody else is living my life.

Mustak's place in my heart has been carved forever.

His reflections are still alive through Amayra, and that's enough for me.

I am going to Shillong with Amayra next week to relive my life.

Moral of the story

Being a single parent is not an easy role to play. Like **Nkwachukwu Ogbuagu,** rightly said, "Single parenthood is when, like a soccer goalkeeper, you're compelled to guard two goalposts at the same time."

There might be financial constraints due to single income, leading to a struggle for that parent to put healthy food on the dinner table, resulting in them having to work overtime/ insane hours resulting in deterioration of not only their physical and mental health but also affecting their family life, the family which is already broken! They might not be able to spend quality time with their children leading to emotional struggles not only for them but also for their growing children.

On the professional front, there might be the pressure to meet the deadlines, training, learning and development to progress in their careers, promotions etc.

There will be double the demands on your time and energy and you might see yourselves multi-tasking, juggling between yourself, your kids and your work at all the times and within yourself, you don't want to drop anything so as to prove yourselves. Please remember, you are strong enough to tackle everything if you take care of yourself. Do not let yourself bury deep under the ground. We all would want to give the best to our kids but in doing so, do not forget to do the best for yourself too.

I am not suggesting you to go partying with your friends, leaving the children behind alone at home but I am asking you to:

- Meditate daily/ regularly

- Go out for walk in the mother nature and you can make it a family exercise, take your kids with you too.

- Do physical exercise, whether at home or at gym. Yoga is powerful too

- Write journal daily which will allow you to reflect constructively and will give you time to make decisions easily.

- Cooking/ Baking and gardening with your children to be able to know each other better.

- Bed time conversations with your children, if not possible daily, make sure its happens at least once a week so you are always aware what they are thinking and if they might be struggling with some issues. They will get to know you better too.

- Friends are important in life, have some trustworthy friends with whom you can open up with your feelings and emotions as you might feel drowned more than others managing a single person household singlehandedly. True friends are the best counsellors.

"Just because I am a single mother doesn't mean I cannot be a success." - Yvonne Kaloki

"I can't tell you how much I respect all the single parents out there doing it solo" #Jennie Finch

'Single Parent': A poetic message from our home Poet

When a couple is torn apart,
Their paths fall apart,
When a relationship crumbles,
The life of both dwindles.

Lives are destroyed,
Lives are three,
Hubby is the first,
Wife is the second,
The child is the third.

They don't know who is impacted,
Their child is the one who is impacted,
His development is being impacted,
He wants his parents to be compacted.

If you are a dad,
He will search for his mom,
If you are a mom,
He will search for his dad,

As a sequel,
Mom-Dad equal,
Mom also becomes Dad, if a Dad leaves,
Dad also becomes Mom, if a Mom leaves,

In my opinion, both are thieves,
Robbed a childhood, these thieves.

Dad also plays,
The Mom's role,
Mom also plays,
The Dad's role,
The only thing that doubles,
Are their roles, are their roles.

Happiness on their face disappeared,
Burden on their face swiftly appeared,
Happiness is chased by the child,
A smile on his face is missed by the child.

To spread happiness,
One should be jolly,
They search for happiness,
As children are jolly.

This is my message,
To a single parent,
They should be proud of,
Being a single parent.

CHAPTER 13 :

BLESSED WITH BEAUTY, DISGUISED BY DESTINY

"However, motherhood comes to you, it's a miracle!".
#Valerie Haper

Snapshot

You're not blessed with everything. Be content with what you have.

The same happened with Gayathri and Abhay. They were happy, but their family wanted more happiness because now their happiness lies in their grandchild.

Forcing or questioning a couple, "do you have kids? It's been a long time since you guys are married and still have no kids?"

These questions are personal, and respect others' feelings. You never know that asking such questions and pressurising a couple for a kid is not normal.

It may lead to conflicts, separation and other ill effects among the couple, but Gayathri and Abhay were different. They know that infertility is nothing to be ashamed of.

They talked about it and realised that even medical treatments didn't work for them, and they're not blessed with it naturally, so they opted for adoption.

It's about accomplishment, not target fulfilment.

Character Sketch

Character Description

Gayathri is in her late 20s. She is tall, slim and has a wheatish, glowy skin tone. Gayathri has black kohled eyes and thick black, shiny straight hair.

She loves putting flowers in her hair as an accessory. Gayathri is a confident and robust lady.

Story

It was Abhay's parents' 30th wedding anniversary. I was excited as it was the first function after my marriage at my in-law's house.

We chose our garden area for the party, with a white and blue decor theme and colourful fresh flowers.

The guests start arriving. Abhay and I welcomed everyone. Raashi didi, Abhay's sister, was with my mother-in-law and her daughter on the stage.

Everyone was having their good times, as many of them met at my wedding eight months back. Now happy again to be together.

I asked the event planner, *"It's already late. Where's the cake?"*

He said, *"Look, here it is." Three-tier vanilla and fresh fruit cake."*

And the party began with a cake cutting ceremony; Everyone was happy and cheerful.

Suddenly I was called out by my name Gayathri. I turned back, and there was a group of elderly women who asked, *"Now you're married for eight months; is there any good news?"*

I smiled and replied, *"No, not now. I'm too young, hahaha!*

They all rolled their eyes and passed a sarcastic laugh.

To which Abhay's mother said, *"I got pregnant after two months of my marriage."*

This made me feel uncomfortable, but I said, "Hey! Let's dance on this track. It's my in-laws' favourite song."

Soon after, 15 months after my wedding, my in-laws started pressuring me for a grandchild.

That night I was sitting on my bed, thinking I was just 26 and not ready for a child.

I asked my husband, *"Isn't it a choice when I want a kid or not?"*

Abhay replied, *"Don't worry! I'm with you. We can at least try for a baby. What do you say?"*

I said, *"Okay. But I'm not mentally prepared for this."*

Abhay replied, *"Everything takes time."*

Three months passed, and the results were still negative.

We thought of consulting a doctor without informing our families until the results came.

I was eagerly waiting for our reports, and finally, the result came after a week. Abhay and I were sitting in the car outside the hospital.

I was shivering and started crying. Abhay hugged me and said, *"We're together in this."*

I said, *"Abhay, why only me?"*

I felt shattered when the doctor told me I couldn't conceive naturally. But she gave us hope for advanced medical treatments.

I was scared. Abhay took me to my favourite momo stall to cheer me up. But I know what I've lost without even gaining.

We came back home and decided to tell the truth to our families.

Abhay's mother started crying and saying, *"My son's life is ruined. Please, god, save us from this curse. I didn't know that Gayathri only has a beautiful face but not a beautiful destiny."*

These lines are carved into my heart and mind. Am I a curse? I cried on my destiny.

I said to God, *"I don't want this beautiful face; please, god, I want a beautiful destiny, a child."*

Abhay's sister called me and said, *"Don't worry, many options are available now. You can try that."*

And we decided to go for IVF. It was successful; I conceived, and my little angel Ayaan was born on 25th June 2015.

Ayaan was weak, so he was kept in the NICU for 15 days. The family welcomed Ayaan with a grand celebration. Abhay's mother was showing off her grandson to everyone. He is my Ayaan, our grandchild. He looks like his father only.

Ayan was one month old when he got jaundice. We took him to the doctor, but Ayan died a week later.

It seemed like I was living the best of my dream, and suddenly someone woke me up.

I was lost, devastated, and lost weight but I was least concerned about my appearance because I had lost my world, a part of mine.

Soon when I heard Abhay's mother convincing him about the second marriage. As I was of no use.

Abhay took a stand and said, *"I'll not leave Gayathri, nor marry someone else. This is my final decision."*

I hugged Abhay and cried my heart out. He said it's destiny. We can try again.

I did not have the courage to go for an IVF again. But my family insisted on me and said you're young. Give it a chance.

I got convinced. We have an appointment with a doctor next week.

It was 5:00 am. I opened my eyes and looked at my yoga mat for a minute; then, I looked at my mobile to send a good morning message to Abhay. He went to Bangalore for his official meeting.

I was still in bed, closed my eyes and realised why there is still a stigma that having your own child is important.

I thanked God and realised I have a beautiful destiny, a loving and understanding partner, and a beautiful family. What else do I want?

I decided not to harm my body anymore just to fit in with society.

Abhay replied, "Gayathri, we have an appointment with a hospital next week for adoption."

I couldn't control my happy tears. I got up in the excitement with the hope of seeing a rainbow again.

At the breakfast table, I told my decision to Abhay's family. I'll not go for IVF, nor I'll take any medicines to conceive.

If you all want a grandchild, Abhay and I have decided on adoption. Many eyebrows were raised, but I didn't listen to anyone this time.

Abhay and I started the adoption process.

Moral of the story

Alternatives in case of infertility, same sex marriages or secondary infertility and miscarriages:

Following if you/ your family prefers a child with your own blood:

- Assisted conception (IVF)

- Surrogacy

- Donor Insemination

Or

- Adoption if you want a child, and if blood is not of a primary concern to you.

Or

- To do nothing and accept what may come your way.

Not each of the above options will be right for you, so discuss between yourselves and seek counselling in order to work out the best way forward for you and your partner.

ADOPTION is great due to the following reasons; you will be changing positively more than one life in the process of adoption.

Benefits to the child

- A house to call a home of their own

- Happy childhood

- Access to education and an opportunity to have a bright future

- Emotional support which is more than taking care of their physical needs

- Close family and other social relationships

Other benefits

- There is no upper age limit for adoption unlike Assisted conception.

- You don't have to try Fertility treatments first; Adoption can be a 1ˢᵗ Positive choice if you are unable to conceive.

- You don't have to be a couple to be able to adopt and even your sexual orientation is not important for adoption.

THE ADOPTED CHILD MAY NOT BE THE FLESH OF YOUR FLESH, MAY NOT BE THE BONE OF YOUR BONE BUT STILL WILL BE YOUR OWN LIKE A MIRACLE!!!

For me, Adoption is a blessing, the adopted child might not have grown in the mother's womb but surely this miracle, your delicate bundle of joy, will grow in your hearts to fill your lives with love and laughter!!!!

CHAPTER 14 :

LIFE OUTSIDE THE WINDOW

"The biggest disease the world suffers from in this day and age is the disease of people feeling unloved"   *#Princess Diana*

Snapshot

You're not bound; it's you who creates the boundaries; you can erase them whenever you want.

No matter at what age you become a widow, let's not others decide in which way you have to live or what you have to eat.

Death is destined, but you're not dead yet, so why are widows supposed to live like a dead person?

The same happened with this twenty-three-year-old widow who was captivated in her own house named as a curse.

But this young girl gathered the courage and realised she was not dead; she still had feelings and desires for a beautiful life.

Are we still living in a society where it's easy to blame wives for their partner's death?

Character Sketch

Character description

A 24 years old girl with fair skin tone and a fit body, long layered straight hair with blonde highlights.

She has a perfect cupid bow lips and a celestial nose with a dimple smile.

Story

Before marriage, all colours were happy colours for me. I did not know that one day I would be forced to wear only white for a year.

It's been a long time since I travelled and ate my favourite food or dressed up. Curd and rice were never on my list.

Being 23 years old, I did not know that being a widow is a curse. More than religion, it's a society that kills you.

It has been four months now since my husband's demise. I'm at my in-law's house, and nobody is at home today because they all went to a wedding in Jaipur.

I didn't go because traditionally, it's unacceptable for a new widow to attend a wedding.

After a long time, In the absence of everyone, I used the main kitchen and made a cup of *"Kadak chai and Maggi"* for myself.

Today is my wedding anniversary. I wore my favourite *"Floral Pink Anarkali Suit with a wavy hairstyle and a blush pink Lip Gloss."*

I opened my room's window to feel the February breeze. *"Hair blowing in the wind touching my face gave me a sense of freedom."* It's not that I don't love my husband or I don't miss him. It's just that I'm still alive.

I stepped into the balcony after months where *"Mogra"* was spreading its fragrance like never before.

I clicked some golden hour *"Selfies"*.

I sat on my balcony to talk to myself.

Why do I feel captivated? Do you want to live this *"Bechari"* life?

Are you sure? Because this is not you.

Other people decide my menu. Why?

We live in a modern society. Where still traditions are followed religiously and blindly, and humanity dies within.

I still love my husband, and I am sad without him, but does this mean I need to spend the rest of my life grieving and mourning?

Why was I blamed for my husband's death and bad fortune?

He died because of his hereditary illness, and we all know that. Still?

Isn't it fate?

Isn't it my loss? That I lost my partner, my friend, my love forever.

Does it give satisfaction to blame a woman for her husband's death?

I finished my *"Chai and Maggi"*.

By then, I realised it was time to live again, so I called my in-laws and told them. I'm going to my parent's house. They angrily asked, *"Why?"*

I replied, *"Because I don't feel captivated there"*.

"I hanged the call".

Sun was setting; the sky was pink, flowers were swinging, birds were returning to their nest, and there was peace inside me.

And I was singing, *"Har ghadi badal rahi hai roop zindagi chaun hai kabhi, kabhi hai dhoop zindagi."* (Song from Kal ho Na ho, a Bollywood superhit movie)

I live with my parents now; I'm doing what I couldn't do before. I started working as a freelance makeup artist and living my best.

There is not a single day that I don't miss *"Vivek"*. But my husband taught me to live every day because he knows how it feels to live in fear of death.

"Grief is never ending. Living with the memories, and living in the memories is the choice".

Moral of the story

Being a widow is the big scary truth and there is no such thing as to how to overcome this pain of losing your loving husband forever. The word 'widow' disgusts and your beautiful marriage which used to bring butterflies to your tummy now changed to sand in your mouth and dropping down of your stomach every time it flashes back into the past, into those romantic encounters, into those sweet-sour daily fights and the list goes on.

Off course, you would like to cry. CRY, CRY IT LOUD and let your tears dried out so there is a space only for smile and love in the future. Shed your tears that he is gone, but do not let the society take your shine away with your deceased husband. HE IS DEAD, NOT YOU!

Do not feel that your heart is empty that now he is gone, feel the love you both shared and make it your strength to live your life.

Be happy today and tomorrow, remember yesterday but do not hold on to it forever for you cannot live it back in it.

Cherish his memories, live your life and close your mind to any negativity the society might want to instil in you, around you.

Listen to the messages he is sending from up there, from heaven- he loved you and asking you not to worry about him anymore. He is safe with the God Almighty and he would like you to concentrate on yourself, your future, your life and would like to see you HAPPY, HAPPY AND LIVELY, exactly the way you used to be when he was with you.

STAND UP FOR YOURSELF as you're a living being. Look out not only for your physical wellbeing but also for mental and emotional happiness. Remember not to become a victim of circumstances!!

As Megan Markle said, " You draw your own box. You introduce yourself as who you are…You create the identity you want for yourself."

Do not let them decide on your behalf.

CHAPTER 15 :

LITTLE RAINBOW OF STRENGTH

"I can be changed by what happens to me, but I refuse to be reduced by it."
#Maya Angelou

Snapshot

Be courageous enough to face the world alone.

The story of Prerna is like a nightmare, one she can never forget.

When we're in trouble, we run to our families for help, but what if your own family is killing your soul and asking you to be quiet for your lifetime? Then what place is left to go or hide and feel safe?

Prerna has spent her life in the horror of pain and fear. She was silent in her growing stage when children were carefree and had only homework stress.

Either she would have attempted suicide, or she would've endured all this throughout her life.

But Prerna didn't let anyone decide against her pregnancy. A twelve-year-old child got the strength to fight for her unborn child and face the world alone.

Character Sketch

Character description

Prerna is in her late 40s now and has attractive facial features, big deep eyes, and long healthy hair touching her knees.

Prerna is 5.4ft with a medium body built and a fair complexion; she now wears glasses while reading.

Story

Wolfy, wolfy, Stop! Give my doll back. Look, mom, Wolfy is running in the garden holding my doll with his teeth; how cute he looks.

Wolfy then left the doll on the swing, and suddenly he stopped at the gate and started barking as I turned around to look back; it was my dad with a young boy standing at the gate holding his hand and suitcase.

I ran towards my dad with a doll in my hand and hugged him. Then dad picked me up and hugged me.

I asked dad, *"Who is he, dad, and what's his name?"*

Dad replied, *"He is your elder brother, Vansh."*

I was happy and excited that I got a brother as a present on my 3rd birthday; this was the best gift I could ever ask for.

I shouted, "Mom, mom meet Vansh bhaiya." My mom came out in the garden where she saw me and Vansh bhaiya sitting on the swing, Wolfy on the side, and dad with a suitcase holding my doll.

Mom and Dad were silent and went inside while we were playing outside. After a few minutes, we heard noises coming out of the house.

Mom angrily asked, *"Whose child is he?"*

Dad replied, *"He is my son; let's accept the reality and don't punish my son for my mistake. Everything will be alright."*

My mom became quiet, and after few months, she passed away due to depression. I was too young to be brought up alone by my father. My father decided to send me to my maternal aunt's home.

I was looking from the corner of the wall when my aunt came to take me. I was holding my doll and was wearing a blue dungaree.

I was 3.5 years old, and bhaiya was seven when I went to my aunt's place, where I never felt far away from my house. They loved me and took care of me like a princess.

When I turned nine, my aunt realized it was time I should go back to my father's house, so I didn't lose connection with my father. I was happy to live with my father and bhaiya again.

We returned to Jaipur from Delhi, and I started living with my family. My father and brother were happy to see me again; I enrolled in a new school and met my old friend Naina there.

A year passed by, and I turned 10. My father married again to give us the love of our mother. I was happy and spread this news among my friends as a rose fragrance that I got my mother back.

Our new mother was fine to me but much nicer to bhaiya. I realized it was because I got more attention at my aunt's house. So, our relationship will become smooth with time.

Our summer vacation was about to start in a week, and I was standing on the balcony thinking I would go on a family vacation this year. Then suddenly my brother came from behind and grabbed me in a strange way.

I felt the discomfort, and without saying anything, I walked off. My parents went out for grocery shopping when my brother came into my room and touched me inappropriately.

I said, *"Bhaiya stop it. What are you doing?"*

He kissed me on my lips forcefully and said, *"just be quiet."*

I was scared and confused as I was only ten years old. The next day I told my mother about this incident.

She said*, "You're thinking wrong; Vansh is your brother; he can't do anything wrong with you, and don't tell this to your father."*

I became quiet. My schools were closed. I couldn't share this with all my friends.

It started with molestation and then he raped me every day, every single day in my own home. No one heard my screams as he always used to put his hands on my mouth. And I was losing myself with each passing day.

I told my mother again as I was hesitant to share this with my father. She said, "Prerna *you must have done something wrong to arouse his desires.*"

I was shocked by the response of my mother. I spent those two months in fear and pain.

My school reopened, and my friends realized I was quieter than before; Naina insisted on knowing what was troubling me.

I told her about every pain of mine. She encouraged me to tell this to my father and show the real face of Vansh and my stepmother.

That night I gathered the courage to tell this to my father, but he ignored all my talks.

I felt disheartened and cried day and night. That moment is still not blurred and shook me completely.

I started losing my confidence, happiness, and peace. This continued for two years, and I became pregnant, but my family decided to abort the child. I heard their conversation that night, and instead of going to school, I went to the police station the next day and told the officer everything in detail.

I was kept in a child health care centre till my pregnancy, and at the age of thirteen, I gave birth to my little rainbow of strength, "*Viaan.*"

Viaan's birth was a turning point in my life when I held my life's decisions without being in fear.

I never went back to my father's house. After that, I went back to Delhi and stayed at my aunt's place and raised Viaan there. I met somebody when I was in my second year of graduation. He accepted Viaan and me wholeheartedly, and Ravi never made it feel like Viaan was not his son.

After that, I never looked back at my family. It'll take forever to get out of that trauma, but I didn't stop there; I told the world about what Vansh did.

Vansh is still not guilty; married and a father of two children. We're all at our respective places. But I do not regret giving birth and raising my child. That was something that encouraged me to face the world without fear.

Ravi and I are happy with our family. Ravi has supported me in whatever I am today, and I wish pain to Vansh for his lifetime.

Moral

CHILD SEXUAL ABUSE is a hideous crime and it happens when a child is forced to take part in sexual activities through physical contact or a non- contact activity online or otherwise.

Effects on the victim

- Post-traumatic stress disorder (PTSD)

- Anxiety

- Panic attacks, flashbacks and nightmares

- Depression

- Intimacy issues with their partners later in life affecting their love life

- Unstable relations

- Can negatively affect the development of a child's brain by weakening cognitive development

Signs and indicators of child abuse

- A child is afraid/ anxious/ fearful/ shivering/ uncomfortable around a particular family member/ friend.

- Bruising

- Bleeding/ Discharge

- Pain/ Soreness in the genital or anal area

- Pregnancy at a young age & STD's

- Bed wetting

- Self-harm

- Eating disorders

- Sleeping disorders and nightmares, waking up at night shouting (nightmares)

- Sexualised behaviour or sexual knowledge which is inappropriate for their age

- Referring to 'secrets'

- Running away from home

- Scared to be alone

- Social anxiety

These signs and indicators are also the effects of sexual abuse and most of these stay for the life time, it haunts the victimised child throughout their life, so we need to STOP it by spreading more social awareness.

Who are the predators/ offenders?

- Close/ distant family members

- Friend

- An adult who found and targeted them as their potential victim, who have gained unsupervised access to the young children to groom the child.

What it may look like to others and the victimised child?

- An older family member taking too much care of a particular child which may look normal to others but there could be physical, emotional or financial power this older person might be exercising on the child to give execution to their dirty intentions.

- The 'partner' 'boyfriend' model where this abuser grooms the child by exchanging gifts, nude photos and through other more normal dating activities making the child believe it to be a 'NORMAL' relationship and get themselves involved in this hideous crime voluntarily.

- Organised which is also known as 'child trafficking' where children may be abused collectively as part of a network resulting not only in the national/ international movement of the victim but also exchanging nude images of the victim.

How to RESPOND to it?

- Contact the police immediately to express your concerns

- Contact your local child protection services (check out the website of the local authority of the victim child's residency area)

- Contact the NSPCC helpline who are trained and professionals to support you and will be able to give you their expert advice to save your child.

- The above are not listed in a natural order and hence use as per the severity of the situation.

- Do not ignore child's point of view as most of the child abuse happen as they are not believed by their adults and they've to bear the pain of this abuse throughout their life.

- Make it clear to the child that their abuse was not their fault at all, they fell in as the prey of a sick and a cruel person.

- Do not ask Direct questions as children might not know what/ how to respond, look out for those unspoken words and their body language.

- Children should know 'Good touch' and 'Bad touch' from the very young age and should be aware of the fact that their private parts are supposed to remain private and should not be infringed.

- Train/ educate the kids more about what could be 'Sexual abuse'

- Tell them to watch out for the possible sexual abuse and to speak about it if they notice something unusual.

IGNORING SEXUAL ASSAULT IS NOT OK!

YOU NEED TO TELL YOUR STORY SO AS TO INSPIRE OTHERS AND IF YOU WILL NOT SPEAK UP, NO ONE ELSE WILL!!!!

CHAPTER 16:

CINDERELLA LOST HER PRINCE CHARMING

''You are the master of your destiny. What you make of your life depends only on you''.   *#TexilaAmericanUniversity*

Snapshot

It's better to express than to regret.

That's what Suman did; she kept quiet when it was required. She could have fought with her parents, or her parents could have realised what they were doing was wrong, but instead, they chose their pride over any relationship.

Suman thought she was ugly as she is dark; does darkness decides beauty standards? No. It's just a mindset of society.

Suman was living the best of her life, but she lacked the confidence to express her emotions as she was fed with ugly thoughts.

She was surprised that she had been blessed with a Prince of her life, Arun.

Arun was way too expressive, but Arun could have chosen some other way to express his emotions, love and feelings to Suman than to poison himself.

Suman's life took a roller coaster ride, and it took her a decade to be expressive and vocal about her thoughts.

Character Sketch

Character Description

Suman is in her early 50s, a fun-loving woman who loves to smile and make others laugh with her talks.

She is 5.2 ft, a chubby woman with medium straight hair, a loud voice, and a wheatish skin tone.

Suman is a package of positive vibes and happiness now.

Story

I was at home that day; It was four o'clock, and I asked Sunita to make tea for me when someone knocked on the door.

"Sunita, look who's at the door?"

Sunita, *"Madam, It's a postman."*

I was sitting in my room on my rocking chair, waiting for my tea, and Sunita was listening to an old Bengali song on her phone. My balcony door was open, the curtain was blowing with a light cool breeze, and I could see my roses.

Sunita brought a cup of tea, butter biscuits and a wedding card on a tray. She kept the tray on my coffee table and said, *"Madam postman gave this wedding card and then she left the room."*

I saw the name on the wedding card, and the tears couldn't stop rolling down my cheeks.

It was my elder daughter Ankita's wedding card. As I opened the card, I remembered the first time I held Ankita in my arms, and Arun was on cloud nine. He kissed me on the forehead in happiness that he is a father now.

I was Arun's Wheatish Indian Cinderella. I married Arun when I was only eighteen, and Arun was nineteen. I was timid and less educated, but Arun accepted me without any condition.

Within a year, Arun and I welcomed Ankita into the world. Our life was like a fairy-tale, but you know fairy tales are like beautiful dreams, and you've to wake up from them someday.

My in-laws were like angels. Maybe I was not thankful to God, or I was too shy to accept the love so boldly.

Arun and I were just teenagers. I lacked that sense of affection to make me realise his love; Arun had poison, and Ankita was just eleven months old; I didn't know that Arun would leave me like a twinkling star.

I was grieving Arun's death when my parents came to my in-laws' house and told my in-laws to get me married to my brother-in-law. To which my in-laws said 'No' as my brother-in-law loved someone else and he was too young to get married at that time.

My parents were orthodox because I was a young widow. They wanted me to get married to a bachelor.

My in-laws said that they'd treat me and my daughter Ankita as their own, to which my parents said no, we're not taking Ankita; we're just taking our daughter Suman with us.

To which my in-laws were shocked and tried to convince my parents who did not want to listen to anything my in laws had to say, but I couldn't say anything. I left Ankita, a piece of mine and followed my parent's instructions, and within a year, they found a bachelor guy for me in Meerut, and I got married to Laxmikant.

Laxmikant is a man full of greed to marry a widow with a rich family background; My parents loaded Laxmikant with a dowry, but still, his greed didn't end. He treated me like a slave, a money-making machine; he used to ask me to get money from my family all the time.

With Laxmikant, I have two beautiful children, my daughter Disha and a son Siddhu. Every day he made me realise that I'm a widow. He married me just for money.

My struggles started after my second marriage. This time I did not want to lose my children. After ten years of my marriage, I thought of doing something to help my family financially as my second husband didn't do any work. I took a loan from my brothers to start my tiffin service, where Laxmikant used to deliver, and I used to cook. It was going well but as Laxmikant was the money collector, he stopped giving the money to me and spent all my hard-earned money on himself.

My first business failed terribly. My brothers supported me and established electronic devices shop for me. Laxmikant got involved in that business, too, and he sold each shop item and gulped the money again.

I was facing failures again and again. That day I realised the importance and love of losing my prince charming Arun. There was not a single day that I didn't miss Arun and Ankita, but that loss gave me the courage to stand for myself, and it took me fifteen years to become vocal.

I started my seafood exporting business from Kolkata, and after that, I made boundaries with Laxmikant and told him to stay away from that business.

Today I'm totally a different person, more confident; I can make my own decisions now. I wish I could be like this twenty-eight years ago.

My elder daughter hates me for leaving her. I regret not understanding my first relationship. It would be easy if I blamed my parents for all this, but it was me too.

My daughters are married now, well educated and blessed with beautiful children. My son helps me with my business. Laxmikant and I are still husband and wife, but emotionally we were never.

Again somebody knocked on the door, and I wiped my tears, remembering that time.

Sunita, "Madam, it's Siddhu bhaiya."

By then, my tea had cooled down, and its colour had turned dark.

I said to Sunita, "Make another tea for Siddhu and me. Don't forget to add elaichi this time."

Moral of the story

Women must be able to take and make decisions affecting their life, their health, their future, their children and their dreams. Why is it our parents, husbands and eventually our sons have the power and the privilege to take these crucial decisions on our behalf and why we must accept it with or without our will?

Any decision, whether its life changing or otherwise, it should be us who should be dictating our lives and no one else should. They are obviously important parts of our lives but they are not us, they do not have to live that life, we have to live the life which they try to chose for us though we should have the rights and power to contribute to our development, be it our physical health, emotional and mental well-being or our family life.

There should be equal participation in decision making in all the spheres of life!!

From Suman's story there are 2 lessons to be learnt, one is that we need to sail our own boat and the second is that we should not judge others without knowing the choices they had to chose from. Women sometimes are criticised though they were not the ones who chose the wrong path for themselves like Suman whose parents chose it for her, her mistake was only to get influenced by them as she was not given any power to act otherwise.

No one except her both the children understood her and that is a salute to her powerful upbringing that Disha and Sidhu understand their mother, respect her for her strength and her life is an inspiration for them.

''It's easy to judge

It's more difficult to understand

Understanding requires compassion,

Patience, and a willingness to

believe that good hearts sometimes

choose poor methods.

Through judging, we separate

Through understanding, we grow''.

#Doe Zantamata

FINAL WORDS OF WISDOM CONTRIBUTED BY OUR HOME POET

A VICTIM

A victim can be anyone,
A culprit can be anyone,
That anyone can be a male,
Or anyone can be a female,

If a female can be raped,
A male can be raped,
No matter who is raped,
Rape is rape.

There are crimes, similar crimes,
Mentioned in this book, the other crimes,
A man can be a victim, a victim in it,
Rape is just, an example of it.

No partiality should be there,
No discrimination should be there,
As Themis is blindfolded,
So, gender equality must be there.

We come across many victims,
Having raised their voice, these victims,
So brave are, these victims,
What about the unheard victims?

They all go into a state of depression,
You won't listen, they have an impression,
They end up committing a cowardly thing,
Committing suicide is a cowardly thing.

Provide your ears to unheard ones,
Don't act deaf to those ones,
Render to them, moral support,
As their dear ones, do not support,

A woman lacks without a man,
A man lacks without a woman,
They have a natural lock,
They are birds of a feather flock.

No one is superior,
No one is inferior,
Both have the same duty,
To let their ears is their duty.

To the unheard ones,
To the unheard ones.

Final words of wisdom using Harri Holkeri and Dr Suess quotes

*"Men and women have roles – their roles are
different but their rights are equal"*
#Harri Holkeri

**"You have brain in your head.
You have feet in your shoes.
You can steer yourself, any
direction you chose." # Dr Seuss**

GLOSSARY

Chapter 1:

Baniya - Indian Hindu caste consists of moneylenders and traders usually found in the Northern part of India.

Chapter 2:

Beta / Mera Bachcha - My Baby (Indian parents commonly use this to show their love for their children)

Chapter 3:

Ammi- Mother

Abba/ Abbu- Father

Baarat- Arrival of Indian groom on the wedding day (with the family members and usually with the music, drums and firework)

Chai – Tea

Gharara - It's a traditional Muslim outfit for brides with flared pants and a long Kurta paired with a dupatta and heavy jewellery.

Halwai - Halwai is a person whose profession is to cook traditional sweets and snacks.

Jalebi - popular sweet snack in India and many other Asian and African countries. It is made by deep-frying 'all purpose' flour batter in circular shapes, which are then soaked in sugar syrup.

Joda - Dress (a wedding dress)

Joota Churai - It's a fun ritual in Indian weddings where the bridesmaids hide the groom's shoes, and in return they ask for money from the groom to return his shoes.

Nikah - It's an Islamic marriage contract between a groom and bride.

Poori Sabzi- Traditional Indian dish

Zari work - An intricate work of gold and silver threads woven on the fabric.

Chapter 5

Baba - Father (papa, this word is often used in Indian households to refer to father)

Beta - son/ daughter, child

Amma - Mother

Master Ji - Teacher

Roti - Indian bread

Chapter 6:

Vishwavidyalaya - University

Chapter 7:

Aloo Paratha – Potato Indian bread

Baba - Father (this word is often used in Indian households to refer to father)

Rabi season -It's a growing season in India where crops are sown in mid-November immediately after the monsoons and harvested in Summers.

Sarso - Mustard

Chapter 8:

Bhai – Brother

Banarasi – a fabric named after an Indian city

Kamathipura – A Red light area in India, near Mumbai, known for prostitution

Nyka - A woman who runs the brothel

Chapter 10:

Bhaiya - Elder brother

Chai – Tea

Didi - Elder sister

Kulhad - A disposable cup made up of clay is used for drinking tea and coffee

Chapter 14:

Bechari - Helpless poor girl

Kadak chai - Stronger version of traditional Indian tea.

Mogra - Arabian Jasmine flower

Chapter 16:

Elaichi - Cardamom

Printed in the United States
by Baker & Taylor Publisher Services